IMAGES
of America
CIVIL WAR GRAVES
OF NORTHERN VIRGINIA

On the Cover. In September 1861, Confederate soldiers erected the first Civil War battlefield monument, on the Manassas (Bull Run) battlefield. The monument was built on Henry Hill but did not survive the war. Just eight weeks after the end of the war in 1865, Union soldiers built this monument on Henry Hill "In memory of the Patriots who fell at Bull Run July 21, 1861." (Library of Congress.)

IMAGES
of America

CIVIL WAR GRAVES
OF NORTHERN VIRGINIA

Charles A. Mills

ARCADIA
PUBLISHING

Copyright © 2017 by Charles A. Mills
ISBN 978-1-4671-2422-5

Published by Arcadia Publishing
Charleston, South Carolina

Printed in the United States of America

Library of Congress Control Number: 2016953531

For all general information, please contact Arcadia Publishing:
Telephone 843-853-2070
Fax 843-853-0044
E-mail sales@arcadiapublishing.com
For customer service and orders:
Toll-Free 1-888-313-2665

Visit us on the Internet at www.arcadiapublishing.com

For Gracie.

Contents

Acknowledgments		6
Introduction		7
1.	Alexandria	9
2.	Prince William County	35
3.	Fairfax County	55
4.	Mosby's Confederacy	83
5.	Arlington National Cemetery	91
6.	Other Notable Graves	115

Acknowledgments

I am extremely grateful for the help of the staffs of the Virginia Room of the Fairfax County Library, the Library of Congress, the Alexandria Library Special Collections branch, and the Ruth E. Lloyd Information Center at the Bull Run Regional Library.

I gratefully acknowledge the excellent work done by the Fairfax County Cemetery Preservation Association and the Prince William County Historical Commission in cataloging and preserving so many historic cemetery sites in Northern Virginia. I am indebted to Dr. Pamela Cressey and Alexandria Archaeology for their fine work in documenting and safeguarding Alexandria's historic cemeteries.

I am grateful for the assistance and support of Lynne Garvey-Hodge of the Fairfax County Historical Commission, Susan Gray of the Fairfax City Museum, Sara B. Anderson of the Prince William County Historical Commission, Don Hakenson, Jon Vrana, Mary Lipsey, and Greg Wilson.

Photographs from the Library of Congress are noted as (LOC) and from the author's collection as (AC).

Introduction

In October 1859, abolitionist John Brown seized the federal arsenal at Harpers Ferry, Virginia. Brown had come to lead a slave uprising. On the morning of October 18, a storming party of Marines under the overall command of Alexandria's Robert E. Lee took Brown prisoner. John Brown, charged with "conspiring with slaves to commit treason and murder," was tried, convicted, and hanged in Charles Town on December 2, 1859. The *Alexandria Gazette* proclaimed that "Virginia has been invaded . . . actually, deliberately, and systematically invaded . . . by an organized band of miscreants, white and black, from Free States, under the lead of a Kansas desperado, at the instigation and appointment of influential and wealthy Northern Abolitionists!"

Despite the Brown raid, it was not a foregone conclusion that Virginia would join the Confederacy in 1861. Although South Carolina and six other states in the lower South seceded in late 1860 and early 1861, before the inauguration of Abraham Lincoln, those in favor of preserving the Union were initially in the majority in Virginia throughout the long winter months of 1861. Sentiment shifted abruptly when President Lincoln issued a call for men to suppress the rebellion after the attack on Fort Sumter in April. Fort Sumter fell on April 14, and on the 17th, Virginia adopted an Ordinance of Secession in the form of a repeal of Virginia's ratification of the US Constitution, to take effect upon ratification by the vote of the people. This election took place on Thursday, May 23, 1861, and Virginia seceded from the Union.

Long before the sun rose on Friday, May 24, Union troops were ordered to seize Alexandria and Arlington Heights. By 2:00 a.m., Union soldiers were rowing across the Potomac River toward Alexandria. The entrance of the Federals was unopposed. Slave trader George Kephart went out of business abruptly as the Union army marched into Alexandria. When Federal troops arrived at his slave pen on Duke Street, it was in complete disarray, the sole occupant one old slave still chained to the floor.

On Friday afternoon, miles away at Fox's Mills, north of Fairfax Court House, 17-year-old Sally Summers was minding the afternoon recess in front of her schoolhouse when she saw a surrey coming down the road from the direction of Alexandria. The driver was her uncle, Amos Fox. As he passed he shouted, "You better dismiss your school right away and go home to your mother. The Union army is advancing!"

In June 1861, both sides sent scouting parties into the countryside, with a Union cavalry raid on Fairfax Court House on June 1 and another bloody skirmish at Vienna on June 17. By July, many thought the first battle, about to be fought on the doorstep of the capital, would end the war. A carnival atmosphere arose; people took picnic baskets and headed out to watch. Capt. John Tidball witnessed a "throng of sightseers."

The first major battle of the war was fought at Manassas on Sunday, July 21, 1861, resulting in a rout of the Union army. The Summers family, whose house was in the path of the retreating soldiers, woke up to find bales of blankets and uniforms in the yard, along with barrels of fish and flour and beef tongues, and even a crate of champagne, all left behind in the panic of retreat.

By August, advance elements of the Confederate cavalry were encamped on Munson's Hill within sight of the unfinished Capitol dome in Washington.

As the struggle surged across Northern Virginia during the next four years, the entire region suffered. Crops were trampled. Fences were used for firewood. Livestock was confiscated. Most of the standing trees were cut to supply building materials or facilitate the firing of artillery. Rifle trenches and ammunition bunkers were dug along the ridges and high ground. Barns, outbuildings, and private homes were occupied, damaged, or destroyed to accommodate the needs of the armies.

With the end of the war, the Union army gathered for one last grand victory parade in Washington. Anne Frobel wrote in May 1865:

> Today we see tents and camps spring up in every quarter. Sherman's army coming in. The roads filled with soldiers as far back as we can see through the woods, coming-coming-coming, thousands and tens of thousands. I hardly thought the world contained so many men and the wagons, O the wagons, long lines of white wagons coming by roads and crossroads. . . . Tomorrow there is to be a "grand review" of the "grand" U.S. Army at Washington and great has been the stir of preparation. . . . Rose Hill is literally covered with Sherman's army and such immense numbers of splendid horses and mules.

Many reminders of the Civil War were left behind in this area for future generations to ponder. Also left behind were the graves of those who took part in the tumultuous events of the war. Northern Virginia is a treasure house of history, perhaps more so than any other part of the country. One unique way of experiencing that history is by visiting one of the region's many historic cemeteries. Cemeteries have been called open air museums, and every gravestone has a story to tell. There are some 1,000 cemeteries in Northern Virginia, ranging from small family plots to huge national cemeteries covering hundreds of acres. Many of them contain the remains of Civil War veterans. This book is not meant to be an inclusive survey of every cemetery in the region; rather, it is a presentation of the Civil War history of Northern Virginia through the medium of cemeteries.

A British prime minister, William Gladstone, once said, "Show me a manner in which a nation or community cares for its dead, and I will measure with mathematical exactness the tender sympathies of its people, their respect for the laws of the land and their loyalty to high ideals." For the most part, Northern Virginia has done an exceptional job in honoring the dead and preserving the nation's historical legacy.

One

Alexandria

In the 1850s, Alexandria was the commercial center for all of Northern Virginia and boasted a busy waterfront, a commercial canal, and expanding railway traffic. Alexandria took great pride in being the "home town" of George Washington. It was on the steps of Gadsby's Tavern (the City Hotel in 1861) that "Light Horse" Harry Lee declared George Washington "First in war, first in peace, first in the hearts of his countrymen."

Alexandria, with its long history of service to the Union, initially opposed secession. Many citizens would gladly have remained in the Union or remained neutral but were prepared to cast their lot with the Confederacy if it came to war. The tide turned toward secession on April 12, 1861, when South Carolina fired on Fort Sumter and President Lincoln called for 75,000 volunteers to crush the rebellion.

Long before dawn on the morning of May 24, 1861, eight Union regiments crossed the Potomac River and seized Alexandria unopposed. The Confederate troops who marched out of Alexandria in 1861 formed the nucleus of the 17th Virginia Infantry. These men would not see home again until 1865, after encountering many horrors and hardships.

For the next four years, Alexandria was an occupied city, and it became a major supply and rail hub for the Union army. Alexandria also became an important hospital center for the Union army. Four churches and many large houses were converted into hospitals, totaling 14 facilities in all. Facilities were overcrowded and often unsanitary, especially after a major battle.

The citizens of Alexandria were called upon to sign a loyalty oath renouncing the Confederacy. Most residents refused to sign. This made life in the occupied town difficult. Taking out a business license, being on the street after dark, leaving town, and even buying a cemetery plot required proof that an individual had signed the oath. At one point, those who did not sign were threatened with forcible deportation. Between the Union forts on the outskirts of Alexandria and the Confederate forces, the countryside rapidly became a no-man's land.

Virginia seceded on May 23, 1861. Long before dawn on the morning of May 24, eight Union regiments crossed the Potomac to seize Alexandria. Col. Elmer Ellsworth led his men down the empty streets until he came to the Marshall House, a hotel flying the Confederate flag. Ellsworth, followed by his soldiers, went inside, hurried to the roof, and with a knife borrowed from a private soldier, cut down the emblem of rebellion. Ellsworth started back for the street with the flag tucked under his arm. In a shadowy hallway he met the proprietor of the inn, James W. Jackson. Jackson produced a shotgun and killed Ellsworth. Within seconds he was cut down by one of Ellsworth's soldiers. War had come to Virginia. The peaceful farmlands would be red with blood before peace finally came again. (LOC.)

According to a friend, ardent secessionist James Jackson had "obstinate determination . . . stamped on every feature." A coroner's jury at Alexandria found that Jackson "came to his death at the hands of troops of the United States while in the defense of his private property, in his own house." (LOC.)

Colonel Ellsworth, a personal friend of President Lincoln, lay in state at the White House before being sent to New York for burial. James Jackson was initially buried in the Jackson family cemetery in Fairfax County. He was later reburied next to his wife, Susan, and other family members in the Fairfax City Cemetery. (AC.)

Colonel Ellsworth became a cult figure in the North. Sermons, editorials, songs, and poems praised the hero. Babies, streets, and even towns were named after him. Enlistments in the army soared. A New York regiment called "Ellsworth's Avengers" quickly filled. Corporal Francis Brownell, Ellsworth's avenger, was lionized and promptly promoted to second lieutenant in the regular Army. (LOC.)

Slaves being sold to cotton planters farther south were brought into Alexandria from the countryside and housed in slave pens until the time for sale. After the sale, they were herded to the Alexandria wharves and shipped out in lots by steamboat. Most citizens of Alexandria accepted the slave trade. (LOC.)

One of the largest and busiest slave pens on Duke Street is pictured here. At night, the slaves were often chained "lest they should overpower their masters, as not more than three or four white men frequently have charge of a hundred and fifty slaves," wrote Ethan Andrews in 1835. (LOC.)

Joseph Bruin, whose grave is pictured, operated a slave jail on Duke Street that still stands today. Bruin gained notoriety in Harriet Beecher Stowe's *Uncle Tom's Cabin*, becoming the model for the greedy slave trader. He was imprisoned during the war and his property confiscated. After the war, he ran a bakery. (AC.)

While many churches were turned into hospitals and stables during the occupation, Christ Church's reputation as George Washington's place of worship preserved it as a church. Union army lieutenant Charles Haydon found Alexandria "A quaint, old looking place. . . . There is not a half hour in the day that I do not have his [George Washington's] presence associated with the surrounding scenery." Lieutenant Haydon mused, "It would do us all good to spend an hour at the grave of Washington in tears over the fate of our country." Union army chaplains conducted services in the church, where a Union army congregation grew up. Most of the original parishioners worshipped with other Southern sympathizers elsewhere. By the summer of 1863, the *Alexandria Gazette* reported that old residents of Alexandria had mostly departed. When the war ended, Christ Church was returned to its parishioners with its interior intact. (LOC.)

Many prominent figures have worshipped at Christ Church. Traditionally, the president of the United States visits Christ Church at least once during his administration. In addition to colonial-era burials, the church cemetery holds the mass grave of 34 Confederate soldiers who died in the local prison camp. (LOC.)

A headstone in the graveyard at Christ Church bears the initials of Union soldiers who left graffiti on graves. George Alfred Townsend, correspondent for the *New York Herald*, wrote, "Many hamlets and towns have been destroyed during the war. But of all that in some form survive, Alexandria has most suffered." (AC.)

15

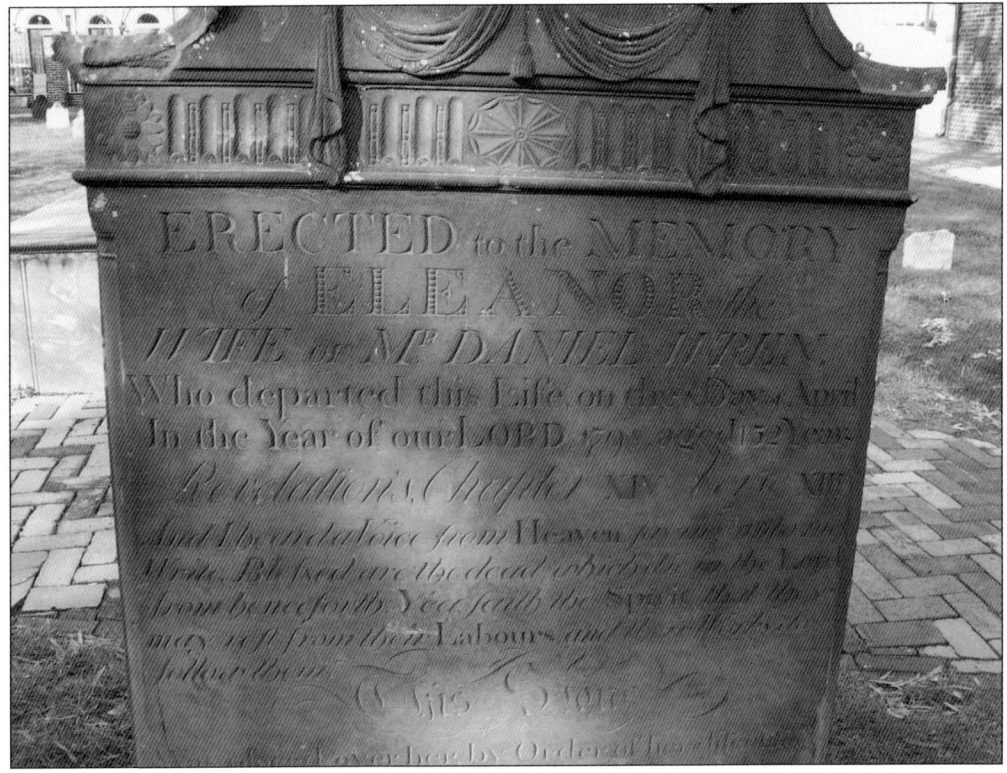

Union soldiers vandalized the grave of Eleanor Wren at Christ Church, changing her age at death from 32 to 132. According to contemporary reports, "The streets were crowded with intoxicated soldiery; murder was of almost hourly occurrence, and disturbances, robbery, and rioting were constant. The sidewalks and docks were covered with drunken men, women, and children, and quiet citizens were afraid to venture [out]." (AC.)

Confederate raiders were a constant danger to the railroads. In October 1864, a number of Alexandria's prominent citizens known to be Confederate sympathizers were forced to ride military trains as human shields. Edgar Snowden Jr., editor of the *Alexandria Gazette*, was one of the hostages. Snowden's grave is seen here. (LOC.)

At the beginning of the war, the Northern states had a population of 22 million. The Southern states had a population of about 9 million (including 3.5 million slaves). The Union fielded some two million soldiers, the Confederacy some one million soldiers (a typical soldier from Virginia is pictured here). Everyone expected the war to be over quickly. The tremendous and growing rush of cotton wealth made the South's pride both brittle and aggressive. The South's explosion of wealth depended on cotton, and the economical production of cotton demanded slavery. A prime field hand could bring as much as $1,500, and his value compounded every time he reproduced. Any Northern move that threatened either cotton or slavery was like a dagger pointed at the heart of the South. (LOC.)

Northern Virginia was not a monolithic society in 1861. Alongside aristocratic families were merchants and small farmers, poor whites, free blacks, slaves, Quakers, and hundreds of enterprising and ambitious Northerners. During the first few years of the war, many parts of Northern Virginia became a no-man's-land in which Union and Confederate troops and sympathizers spasmodically and violently struggled for control. In June 1861, both sides sent scouting parties into the countryside. The first major battle of the war was fought at Manassas on Sunday, July 21, 1861. The Civil War dragged on four long years, becoming the bloodiest war in American history. Some 600,000 people, combatants and noncombatants, died. As a percentage of population, this would be equivalent to seven million deaths in present-day America. Many soldiers were buried where they fell. In an era before identification tags, thousands of soldiers went to unknown graves. (LOC.)

Esther Alden expressed the attitude of many young women in the South as the war progressed: "One looks at a man so differently when you think he may be killed tomorrow. Men whom up to this time I had thought dull and commonplace . . . seemed charming." The famous diarist Mary Chestnut of South Carolina was appalled when she saw women of her own class flirting openly with strangers in public. The diaries of hundreds of women of the time attest to the "marrying craze" sweeping the South. "Every girl in Richmond is engaged or about to be," wrote Phoebe Pember Yates in February 1864. Fear of spinsterhood and natural desire heightened by the immediacy of war led to many unconventional matches, reflecting the truth of a phrase common to the time, "The blockade don't keep out babies." The war left many young widows with small children to raise. (LOC.)

The Union hospital at Fairfax Seminary is seen here. Julia Wheelock came to Alexandria searching for her brother, and after learning of his death, stayed to nurse the wounded. She wrote, "We all went out to Fairfax Seminary Hospital. . . . This is a large hospital and will accommodate several hundred patients. It is situated in a delightful place . . . commanding a fine view of the country for miles around. It was formerly a theological seminary." Patients universally praised the facility, known as the best hospital in Alexandria. Superintendent Jane S. Woolsey ran a crisp and efficient organization that also provided comfort. The well-equipped kitchen prepared dishes for patients on special diets. The seminary housed 1,700 wounded Union troops. Despite the hospital's best efforts, many died. Five hundred soldiers were buried on the grounds. The seminary was founded in 1823. A formal cemetery was established on the grounds in 1876. (LOC.)

The Mansion House Hotel was operated by James Green. In November 1861, Green was given three days to vacate the premises, and the hotel was turned into a hospital. The Mansion House Hospital (featured in the television series *Mercy Street*) was one of the largest military hospitals in Alexandria, with 500 beds. (LOC.)

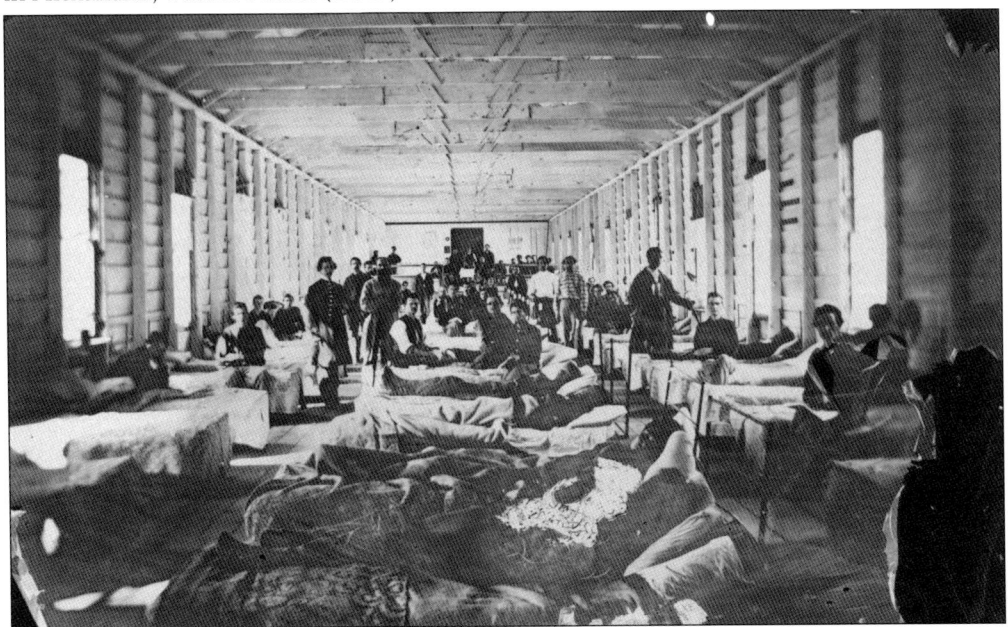

Alexandria National Cemetery was one of the original 14 national cemeteries established in 1862. The first burials were soldiers who died during training or from disease in the numerous overcrowded hospitals around Alexandria (the ward of a typical Union hospital is pictured here). By 1864, the cemetery was nearly filled to capacity. (LOC.)

Alexandria National Cemetery was first known as the Soldier's Cemetery. There are 3,533 Civil War veterans buried here, including 123 unknown soldiers and 229 African Americans who were members of the US Colored Troops. The original wooden headboards were replaced by marble headstones in 1876. (LOC.)

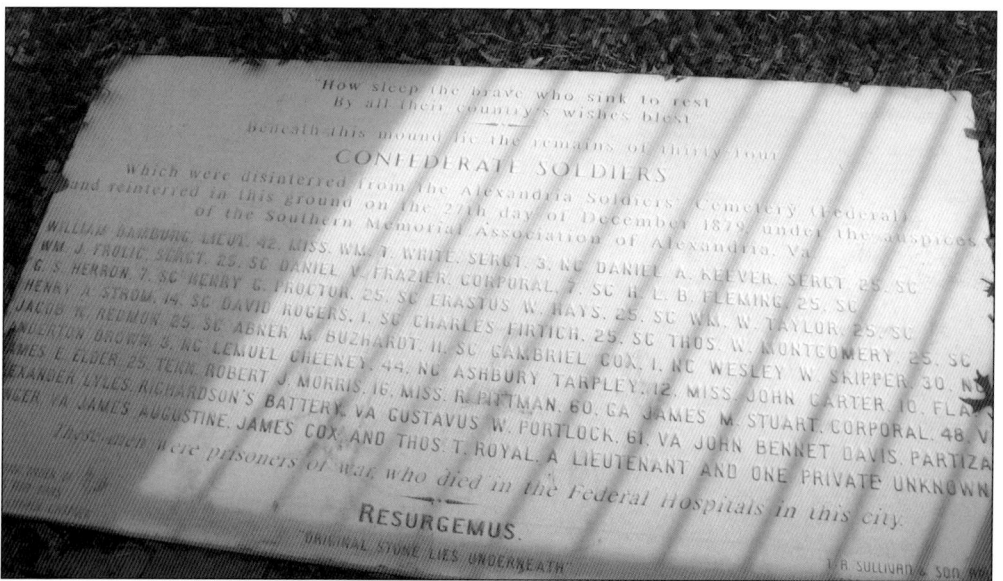

Thirty-nine Confederate soldiers were interred at Alexandria National Cemetery during the war, but most were moved in 1879 to Christ Church Cemetery in Old Town. A marble plaque with the names of the fallen marks the mass grave. The Confederate fallen were remembered for their "courage, fidelity and patriotism." (AC.)

Julia Wheelock wrote this account of a funeral at the Soldier's Cemetery: "We had gone but a few steps when . . . we saw a soldier's funeral procession approaching, a scene I had never witnessed, but one with which I was destined to become familiar. . . . He is escorted to his final resting place . . . by comrades . . . with unfixed bayonets, and arms reversed, keeping time with their slow tread and solemn notes of the 'Dead March.' " (LOC.)

On June 17, 1863, Pvt. Lewis Bissell recorded a funeral procession en route to Soldier's Cemetery. "The ambulances, seventeen in number, each with two coffins, were followed by officers and men. They marched to mournful music played by the First Connecticut Artillery band. . . . It was a sad sight to see the procession move towards the soldier's graveyard in Alexandria." (LOC.)

Nathaniel Shoup of Company C, 84th Pennsylvania Infantry Regiment, is pictured here in uniform. Shoup was born in 1842, enlisted on October 1, 1861, and died of typhoid fever in Alexandria on June 29, 1862. He is buried at the Alexandria National Cemetery, Gravesite No. 59. His gravestone reads "Nath'l Shoup, Sgt. Pa." (LOC.)

Before the ambrotype photograph of Nathaniel Shoup was donated to the Library of Congress, Christian Liljenquist (seen here with the photograph of Shoup) went to Shoup's gravesite at Alexandria National Cemetery. Shoup's regiment lost 224 men during the war: 125 died as a result of battle, while 99 died of disease. (LOC.)

24

In April 1862, President Lincoln emancipated all slaves in the District of Columbia, and nine months later, he issued the Emancipation Proclamation. Many blacks from nearby states sought refuge in Alexandria. Those who came under Union control were known as "contraband of war." (LOC.)

Thousands of freed slaves looked for safety around Alexandria. Blacks were a novelty to many Northerners who had never seen an African American before reaching Virginia. Alexandria provided just what they needed, according to the *Alexandria Gazette*: protection, plenty of work at a fair price, and punctual payment. Only 25 names were on the charitable ration list. (LOC.)

The army built barracks for freedmen. The Union military established L'Overture Hospital as a place where sick and wounded African American soldiers and freed slaves could be cared for. The hospital covered most of the city block at Prince and West Streets. Construction workmen found bones from amputated limbs here in 1879. (LOC.)

The federal government was the main employer of Alexandria's free blacks and former slaves. Many worked for the US Military Railroad and as stevedores on the government docks for the Office of Commissary Subsistence, which distributed food, coal, and hay. By 1864, the contraband population in Alexandria had grown to 7,000. A typical worker is seen here. (LOC.)

The Freedmen's Cemetery on South Washington Street in Alexandria was created during the Civil War as a burial place for former slaves fleeing the Confederacy and flocking to Alexandria. African American soldiers fighting in the Union army were also buried here, but these soldiers were reburied at the newly created Alexandria National Cemetery. This image was found in Cecil County, Maryland, and the unidentified soldier, pictured with his wife and daughters, probably belonged to one of the US Colored Troops regiments raised in Maryland. Over time, the wooden markers memorializing the dead at the Freedmen's Cemetery decomposed. In the 1930s, the George Washington Memorial Parkway was built over part of the graveyard. Construction of the Beltway destroyed the southern edge of the cemetery. In 1955, a gas station was built on top of the graves. (LOC.)

The cemetery was rediscovered by archaeologists and historical researchers in the activity surrounding the expansion of the Woodrow Wilson Bridge and was purchased by the City of Alexandria in 2007. On May 12, the site was rededicated as the Freedmen's Memorial Park. Alexandria Archaeology identified the locations of more than 500 of the 1,800 graves once located in the cemetery. No grave could be associated with a particular person. A wooden picket fence once surrounded the cemetery, and the Army Quartermaster Corps supplied wooden headboards at the time of burial. Each headboard was whitewashed and had the name of the deceased written in black lettering. Several graves had stone markers supplied by the families. A fragment of one stone marker was found during excavation. The graves were placed very close to one another in orderly rows. Gravediggers were probably unaware that they were digging into an important Native American site. A 13,000-year-old spear point was recovered here in 2007. (AC.)

Although the size and tempo of railroad operations greatly increased during the war years, even before the war, Alexandria was home to the Smith & Perkins Locomotive Works. The company manufactured engines for the Manassas Gap, Baltimore & Ohio, and Hudson Valley Railroads. Smith & Perkins Locomotive Works employed some 200 skilled industrial workers. Alexandria was also home to other industries, such as machine shops and foundries. Later in the war, freight cars were built in Alexandria for use by the Union army in the western theater of operations. In the spring of 1865, a private railroad car was built for President Lincoln's personal use. This car was the Air Force One of its day. Ironically, this special presidential car was used for the first time as a funeral car to take the slain president back to his home in Springfield, Illinois. (LOC.)

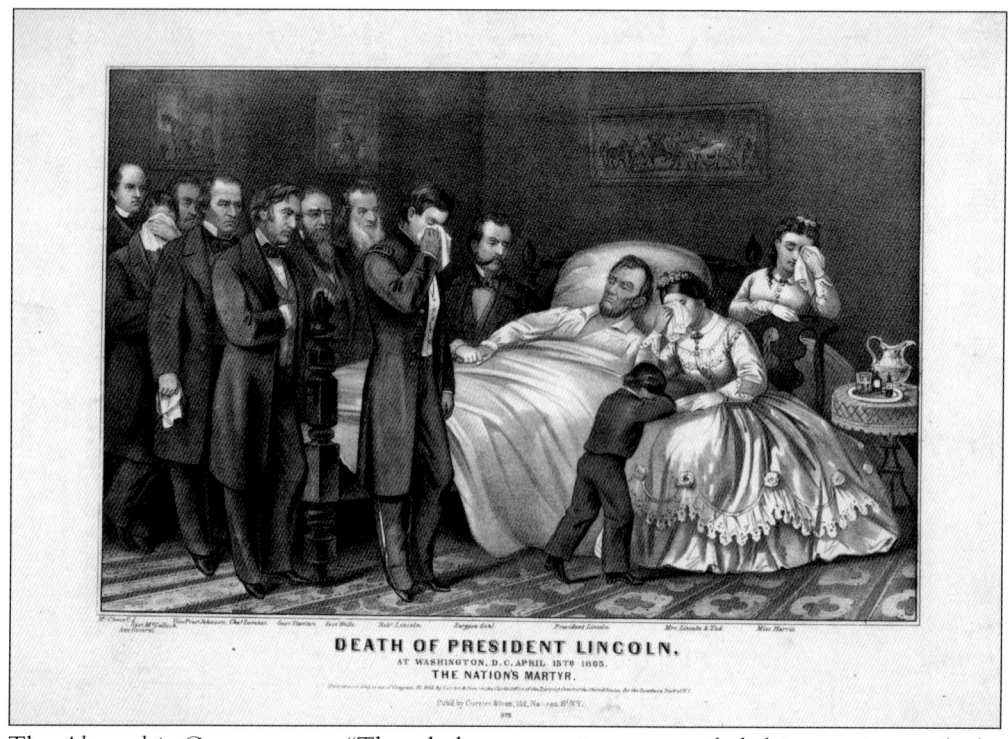

DEATH OF PRESIDENT LINCOLN.
AT WASHINGTON, D.C. APRIL 15TH 1865.
THE NATION'S MARTYR.

The *Alexandria Gazette* wrote: "The whole community was startled this morning, early, by reports from Washington, of the murder of the President of the United States, and the attempted assassination of the Secretary of the State and his son. So astounding was the intelligence, the rumor was at first discredited. No one believed that such a tragedy did or could happen." (LOC.)

Lincoln's funeral train, seen here with funeral bunting, left Washington on April 21, 1865, and retraced much of the route Lincoln had traveled as president-elect in 1861. The nine-car *Lincoln Special*, whose engine displayed Lincoln's photograph over the cowcatcher, carried approximately 300 mourners. Depending on conditions, the train usually traveled between 5 and 20 miles per hour. (LOC.)

A few weeks before his election, Lincoln received a letter from a young girl named Grace Bedell urging him to grow a beard. By the time of his inaugural journey from Illinois to Washington, DC, by train, he had a full beard. The trip took him through New York State and included a stop in Bedell's hometown, where he stopped to thank her for the suggestion. (LOC.)

Embalming came into its own during the Civil War. President Lincoln was assassinated on April 14, 1865, but his body was not interred in Illinois until May 4. The passage of the body home for burial was made possible by embalming and brought the possibilities of the process to the attention of a wider public. (LOC.)

31

Northern Virginia had a diverse population even in 1861. This grave at the Wilkes Street Cemetery Complex is that of a Union man who died during the siege of Petersburg in 1865. (AC.)

Montgomery Dent Corse (1816–1895) served as a brigadier general in the Confederate army, commanding the 17th Virginia Infantry and then Corse's Brigade of Pickett's Division in the Army of Northern Virginia. Corse participated in many important battles, but his brigade was not at Gettysburg during Pickett's fateful charge. He is buried at St. Paul's Cemetery. (AC.)

William H. Dulany is buried at St. Paul's Cemetery. Dulany was a delegate to the Virginia Secession Convention in 1861. He served as a captain in the 17th Virginia Infantry and was badly disabled during the First Battle of Manassas. Dulany was a member of the Virginia State Senate from 1863 to 1865. (AC.)

The tombstone of Launcelot Minor Blackford at Ivy Hill Cemetery captures a wealth of biographical information, including his service in the Confederate army and his long tenure as the principal of the Episcopal High School in Alexandria. It also captures the essence of the man: servant of the Lord, gentle, patient, and an apt teacher. (AC.)

Harold Snowden (son of Edgar Snowden) served as a surgeon in the 17th Virginia Infantry. Later, he was a surgeon and an editor of the *Alexandria Gazette*. He is buried in the Wilkes Street Cemetery Complex. The epitaph on his tombstone reads, "He Stood Four Square to Every Wind That Blew." Edgar Warfield, one of Snowden's comrades in the 17th Virginia, wrote of his return to Alexandria after the surrender at Appomattox: "the four of us separated, each to make his way to that home that we had left four years before. I was delayed so much between the wharf and home by the friends I met on the way that on reaching the intersection of King and Water [now Lee] Streets, I turned up the latter street, and then made my way through Smoot's Alley to Fairfax Street. . . . We four were the first arrivals from the surrender at Appomattox." Warfield became Alexandria's oldest surviving Civil War veteran, dying in 1934 at the age of 92. He is buried in Ivy Hill Cemetery in Alexandria. (AC.)

Two

Prince William County

In the 1840s and 1850s, the national debate over slavery enraged Virginians. Issues such as the return of runaway slaves and the extension of slavery into new territories locked Congress in bitter debate month after month. In the spring of 1859, the abolitionist John Brown made a raid on the federal arsenal at Harpers Ferry, Virginia, with the intention of fomenting a general slave insurrection. Harpers Ferry was less than 50 miles from Manassas Junction. The insurrection became the principal topic of conversation. It had come too near home for county citizens not to feel an acute interest.

While all was not well in the land, progress and prosperity characterized the scene around Manassas Junction. The year 1859 was an excellent one for crops. Land was selling for a whopping price. People were justly proud of the rail lines that opened up vast new markets and put them in touch with the latest trends. The shrill cry of the locomotive was welcomed as the harbinger of all that was modern. Little did these peaceful farmers dream that the newly constructed railroad junction would also bring to them the horrors of war.

In 1860, there were 125 households in the vicinity of the newly built railroad center at Manassas Junction. Many of these households were linked by blood or marriage. Kinship was a central concern of these Virginia farmers. Marriage, remarriage, and intermarriage among neighboring families had created extensive family ties. Most of the 548 whites and 45 free blacks were farmers or farm laborers. Most of these belonged to the class of small farmers who tilled their own fields, usually without any help except from their wives and children. In Virginia, only 25 percent of the landowners were slaveholders. Membership in the planter class required ownership of at least 20 slaves. Eighty-eight percent of all Virginia slaveholders had fewer than 20 slaves; 50 percent held fewer than five slaves. The largest slaveholder in the area was William Weir of Liberia plantation, who owned some 80 slaves.

It was a time of straightforward tasks and simple pleasures. On Sunday, families would lay aside farm chores and open the big family Bible. In the afternoon, there were long walks to the home of a neighbor. After a simple supper, many families would gather around the piano and sing hymns. (LOC.)

The Civil War came to Wilmer McLean's kitchen in Manassas on July 18, 1861, when a Union shell dropped down the chimney and exploded in a pot of stew. McLean moved his family to central Virginia, only to have his house chosen for the site of Robert E. Lee's surrender in 1865. The McLean house at Appomattox is seen here. (LOC.)

Wilmer McLean left Northern Virginia in March 1862 and moved to Appomattox Court House. From his experience as a merchant, he knew that a long war would cause the price of commodities to rise higher and higher. He began to speculate in sugar and made a tidy income during the war. After the war, the McLean family returned to the Manassas area virtually penniless. Wilmer McLean still owned many hundreds of acres in Prince William County, but the land was virtually worthless for resale and McLean was heavily in debt. Eventually the ever-practical McLean turned his attention to politics, joined the Yankee Republican Party, supported Ulysses S. Grant in the election of 1872, and was rewarded by an appointment to a US Treasury job. Wilmer McLean died on June 5, 1882, and is buried in St. Paul's Cemetery in Alexandria. (AC.)

Union cavalry is pictured at Sudley Springs Ford. Confederate general P.G.T. Beauregard posted a proclamation on June 5, 1861, that read, "A restless and unprincipled tyrant has invaded your soil. Abraham Lincoln, regardless of all moral, legal, and constitutional constraints, has thrown his abolitionist hosts among you, who are murdering and imprisoning your citizens, confiscating and destroying your property, and committing other acts of violence." (LOC.)

Services were abruptly cancelled at Sudley Church near Manassas when Union troops began crossing nearby Sudley Springs Ford on the morning of Sunday, July 21, 1861. The building became a Union army field hospital. The diarist Maj. Sullivan Ballou of the 2nd Rhode Island Regiment was among those who died at Sudley. (LOC.)

Boys kneel at a crude battlefield grave near Sudley Church. Most soldiers in the Civil War died of disease rather than wounds received in battle. For many, army life was the first time they had come in proximity to large groups of people, and they had no immunity to diseases such as chicken pox, smallpox, scarlet fever, measles, and mumps. (LOC.)

Pictured is the battlefield at Manassas. For days, Southern troops had been massing. Finally, on July 16, the Union army marched out of Washington to meet the Confederates at Manassas Junction. On July 21, 1861, the two armies grappled in the first great battle of the Civil War. (LOC.)

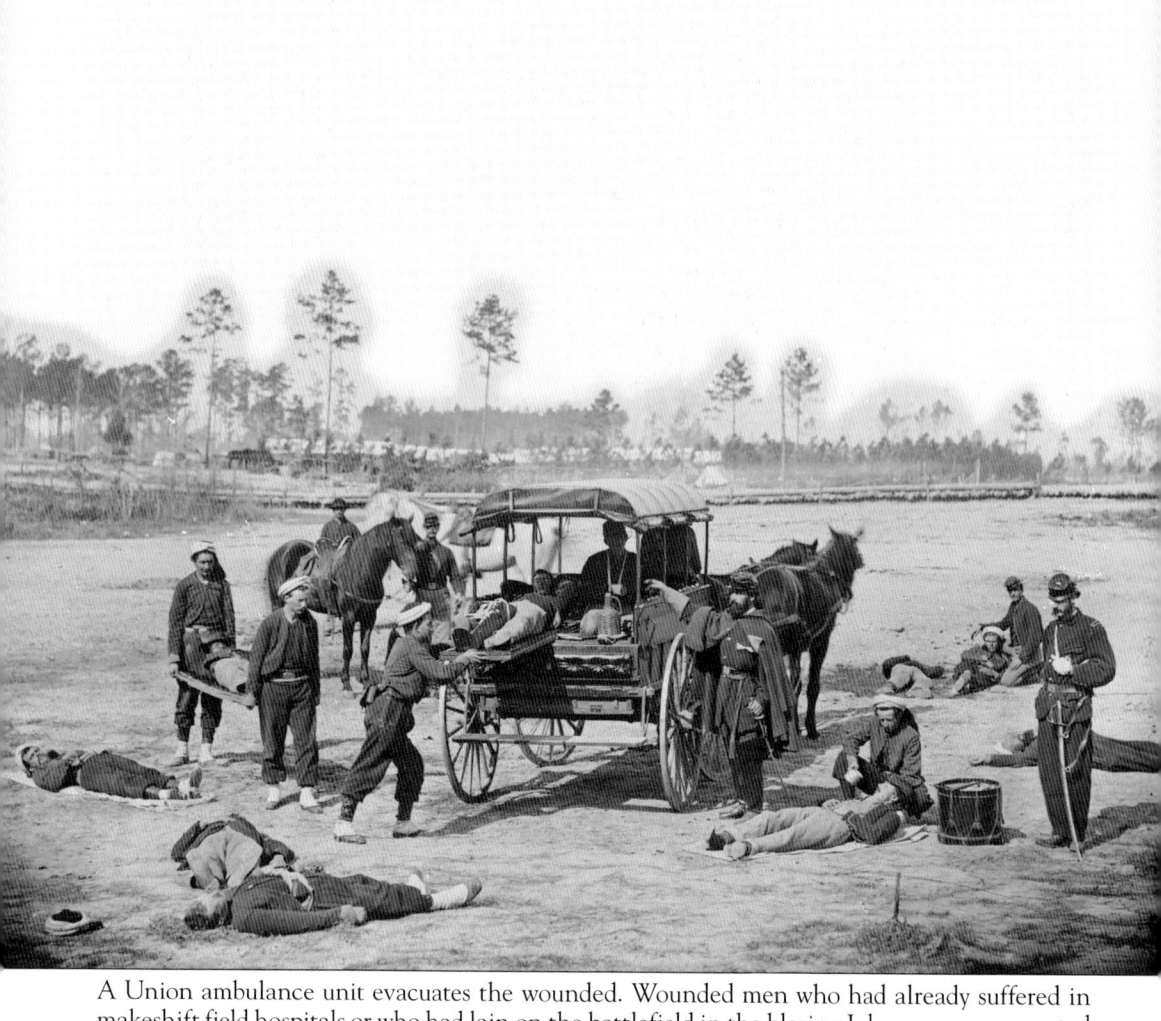

A Union ambulance unit evacuates the wounded. Wounded men who had already suffered in makeshift field hospitals or who had lain on the battlefield in the blazing July sun were evacuated in crude wagons. Railway companies did not have ambulance cars, so freight cars were used to transport wounded Confederate soldiers. Injured soldiers were crowded onto the bare floors of the cars. Most of the wounded were treated within the first 48 hours. Emergency medical care on the battlefield consisted of bandaging a soldier's wounds as fast as possible and giving him whiskey and morphine, if necessary, for pain. Primary care took place in field hospitals. The most common battlefield operation was amputation of arms and legs. Amputation was a quick and reliable answer to the severe wounds created by the .58-caliber minié ball used during the war. (LOC.)

When President Lincoln called for 75,000 volunteers in April 1861 to put down the rebellion, Rebel jokers published advertisements for "75,000 Coffins Wanted." Bill Arp, a popular Georgia humorist, wrote a letter to President Lincoln thoughtfully worrying that the Union's military strategy might be "too hard upon your burial squads and ambulance horses." The First Battle of Manassas, a Confederate victory, was fought on July 21, 1861. July 22 dawned through clouds. It drizzled early, and in the afternoon rained heavily. Many dead and wounded still lay on the field. The Confederate Ambulance Corps found dead men in every conceivable position—mangled, dismembered, disemboweled, some torn literally to pieces. Some, in their death struggles, had torn up the ground around where they fell. Others had pulled up every weed or blade of grass that was in their reach. Soldiers were often buried in shallow makeshift graves. (LOC.)

Before the Civil War, a freed slave named Jim Robinson operated a drover's tavern. Eventually he was able to purchase his wife and three of his five children and buy several hundred acres of land. The Robinson family continued to work their farm after the war. The farm was sold to the Department of the Interior in 1934 to become part of the Manassas National Battlefield. (LOC.)

Prior to selling their farm, the Robinson family acted as informal stewards of their part of the battlefield, taking Confederate remains to a small cemetery to join an estimated 500 unknown soldiers. The family philosophy was summed up in the phrase "Just remember, these remains belonged to someone's son who did not want to die in this manner." (LOC.)

Eighty-four-year-old invalid Judith Carter Henry lay in her bed as the First Battle of Manassas began. Shells from Union artillery began to fall around the widow's house, Spring Hill (seen here in ruins). A shell burst in the room where she lay. She was buried next to her house. (LOC.)

This is the grave of Judith Henry, the only civilian fatality at First Manassas. Judith Carter was born at Pittsylvania in 1777. She was the daughter of Landon Carter, who inherited the plantation in direct descent from Robert "King" Carter. In 1801, she married Dr. Isaac Henry, one of the first surgeons in the US Navy. (AC.)

On July 21, the Lewis family was notified that their house, Portici (above), would probably be in the line of fire. Fannie Lewis was nine months pregnant and went into labor as the family began to evacuate the house. She delivered her first baby, John Beauregard Lewis, on the battlefield. (LOC.)

After the battle, many homes like Portici and the one seen here became grisly field hospitals. The wounded, dead, and dying covered every floor. There were piles of amputated legs, feet, hands, and arms, all thrown together. At a distance, they looked like piles of corn. The dead were buried in nearby gardens. (LOC.)

The original Henry House was completely destroyed during the war, but the Henry family built a new home on the original site in the 1870s. A stone obelisk on the east side of the house honors the Union dead. Erected in June 1865, it is one of the earliest Civil War battlefield monuments. During the 1930s, Works Progress Administration workers recorded numerous oral histories of longtime area residents. Many local citizens recounted a story that the Henry Hill Monument had been built atop a giant mass grave of Union dead. According to this story, the 27-foot obelisk began to slowly lean as the unstable foundation of human remains settled. This mass grave story appears to be a legend. Historical records from the construction and dedication of the monument refute the widely believed story, although it periodically resurfaces. (LOC.)

Standing some 20 feet tall and built of locally quarried sandstone, the obelisk monument on Henry Hill was erected to commemorate the "Patriots of '61." The construction of the monument took only four days. On June 11, 1865, a dedication ceremony took place, attended by Gen. Montgomery Meigs, Maj. Gen. Orlando B. Wilcox, and Gen. Samuel P. Heintzelman. (LOC.)

After speeches and an artillery firing on Henry Hill, the crowds moved down the road to dedicate another monument near Groveton commemorating the soldiers who fell at the Second Battle of Manassas. The rarely visited Groveton monument deteriorated and crumbled until saved and restored by the National Park Service. (LOC.)

Folly Castle was a house about a mile from Henry House. Early on the morning after the battle, Hugh Henry from Henry House came over, saying his mother had been wounded during the battle and had died in the night. He asked Betty Leachman and her sister-in-law to return with him to prepare Judith Henry's body for burial. Hugh Henry is buried next to his mother. (AC.)

After the war, Hugh Henry rebuilt Spring Hill. He became a teacher and later in life acted as an informal steward and guide over his portion of the battlefield. He placed rough board signs on some of the trees and posts in the farmyard and pastures describing the main sites of interest. Henry died in 1898 at the age of 86. (LOC.)

In March 1862, George B. McClellan devised a strategy whereby the Union army would move down the east side of the Potomac River, cross over into Virginia, and capture Richmond while the Confederate army was still far to the north. The Confederates prepared to counter the new Union offensive, evacuating Manassas and the defensive line along the Occoquan River. (LOC.)

The retreating Confederates left large quantities of supplies behind that were quickly looted by the Federals. Soldiers of the 1st Massachusetts Regiment came upon some fresh graves marked with warnings against disturbing the dead. Instead of bodies, they found new tents, uniforms, well-equipped mess chests, and other equipment. (LOC.)

The remains of nearly 100 Alabamans rest in the Alabama Cemetery at Bristoe. Most of these men died during the winter of 1861–1862 while stationed at Camp Jones, located in the Bristoe area. There are many other cemeteries in the Bristoe area with dead originating at Camp Jones. Nearly 1,000 men died at the camp. (LOC.)

Later in the war, in October 1863, the Confederates attacked Bristoe Station near Manassas without proper reconnaissance. Union soldiers, posted behind the Orange & Alexandria Railroad embankment, mauled two Confederate brigades of Henry Heth's division and captured a battery of artillery. The Confederates retired. Dead Confederate soldiers were buried in mass trench graves where they fell. (LOC.)

Abandoned fortifications crumbled after the war. When peace finally came, the area around Manassas was a scene of utter devastation. There was hardly a house, barn, or church that had not been used as a hospital. The population of Prince William County dropped by almost half and would not reach its prewar level again for nearly 60 years. (LOC.)

Shortly after the Civil War, the US government launched a widespread effort to locate and rebury Union soldiers. By 1870, over 90 percent of Union casualties, almost half of whose identities were unknown, were interred in national cemeteries, private plots, and post cemeteries. No such government effort was made for Confederate dead. (LOC.)

1861—1865
Original Photographs taken by the Government Photographer during the war. Taylor & Huntington, Sole Owners, Hartford, Conn.

No. 918.   **SOLDIER'S SKELETONS.**

When the National Cemeteries were established, the remains of the Union soldiers were disinterred from the hastily made graves on the battlefield and placed in the National Cemeteries; this view shows the work of disinterring the remains.

Battlefields presented gruesome scenes of carnage. Gen. Ulysses S. Grant wrote of a field "so covered with dead that it would have been possible to walk across the clearing, in any direction, stepping only on dead bodies without a foot touching the ground." One observer of mass burials said that bodies were "covered over much the same as farmers cover potatoes and roots to preserve them from the frost of winter; with this exception, however: the vegetables really get more tender care." After the war, the US government sent teams of soldiers to collect the dead from battlefield graves, identify the bodies, and give each a proper burial. The work went on for six years, much of it performed by African American soldiers. Some 300,000 Union soldiers were reburied. This picture, taken during the war, shows the grisly work of disinterring the remains. (LOC.)

After the war, farming resumed around Manassas. Plowing uncovered shallow gravesites. To give these dead a proper resting place, Civil War veteran William Sanford Fewell donated an acre of land as a burial site for the often unknown soldiers. The remains of 250 Confederate soldiers were reinterred in this one-acre section shortly after the war. Nearly all had died from disease. The bodies were recovered from original gravesites on surrounding farms. A 75-foot red sandstone monument, built by J.R. Tillet, was dedicated on August 30, 1889. The speakers at the dedication were Gen. W.H.F. Lee, son of Robert E. Lee, and Sen. John W. Daniel, the "Lame Lion of Virginia." The bronze statue that sits atop the monument was added in 1909 and is titled *At Rest*. In 1874, the Town of Manassas acquired the adjoining land and began a citizens' cemetery. (AC.)

During the First and Second Battles of Manassas, heavy fighting often kept both sides from claiming their dead, and after both battles, the armies had to maneuver quickly. Burial details dug shallow graves where soldiers had fallen. Crude wooden headboards sometimes noted the soldier's name and regiment. Many went to their graves anonymously. Rains soon washed away the thin cover of soil, exposing the remains. A *Harper's Weekly* correspondent wrote, "In the long, luxuriant grass, one strikes his foot against skulls and bones, mingled with the deadly missiles that brought them to earth. Hollow skulls lie contiguous to the hemispheres of exploded shells." The Confederate cemetery at Groveton was established in 1869 by the ladies of the Groveton and Bull Run Memorial Association. At least 266 Confederate dead were reinterred here. The monument to the Confederate dead in the center of the cemetery was dedicated on August 30, 1904. (AC.)

Most of the dead at the Groveton cemetery are unknown. Only two graves have marked headstones: Pvt. William G. Ridley, 6th Virginia Infantry, and Pvt. James J. Palmer, Palmetto Sharpshooters. Both men were killed on August 30, 1862, during the Second Battle of Manassas. The National Park Service acquired title to the cemetery in 1973. (AC.)

Civil War ruins are seen here. The Manassas National Battlefield Park was established in 1940 to preserve and protect the land and resources associated with the First and Second Battles of Manassas. Few places exemplify the problems of historic preservation as urgently as this historic site, which has been regularly encroached upon. (LOC.)

Three

FAIRFAX COUNTY

Fairfax County was a no-man's land during much of the Civil War. Early in the war, Confederate troops occupied most of the county. Union troops occupied the northern and eastern parts of the county, especially near Alexandria. Troops from both sides crisscrossed the area, often wreaking havoc. Several minor engagements occurred early in the war. On June 1, 1861, Union cavalry raided the village of Fairfax Court House. During the raid, Capt. John Quincy Marr was killed, becoming the first Confederate officer killed in the war. Marr became a Confederate martyr. Later in June, fighting broke out at the village of Vienna. Skirmishes were also fought near Dranesville and Centreville. Two major battles, First and Second Manassas, took place just south and adjacent to the county.

After the Union defeat at First Manassas, President Lincoln appointed Gen. George McClellan as commander of the demoralized Union army. McClellan rebuilt the army and staged the largest military review ever held to that point near Bailey's Crossroads.

On September 1, 1862, following Second Manassas, the Battle of Chantilly (also called the Battle of Ox Hill) was fought in Fairfax County. Two Union generals, Philip Kearny and Isaac Stevens, were killed in this battle. After Second Manassas and the Battle of Chantilly, Union and Confederate wounded were brought to St. Mary's Church in Fairfax Station to be cared for by Clara Barton, who later founded the American Red Cross.

Two of the war's most famous cavalry raids happened in Fairfax County. In late December 1862, Confederate general James Ewell Brown "Jeb" Stuart captured supply wagons, Union prisoners, and mules at Burke Station. Stuart sent a telegram of complaint about the quality of the mules he captured to Union quartermaster general Montgomery Meigs. In March 1863, Confederate raider Col. John. S. Mosby captured Union general Edwin Stoughton as he slept in the village of Fairfax Court House.

The war devastated commercial activity in the county. Railroad and telegraph services were disrupted and at times halted. Both sides raided and burned farms. Troops shut down business establishments. Destitute civilians wandered county roads. Discarded military hardware littered the countryside.

The grave of John Quincy Marr is in the Warrenton Cemetery. Before dawn on June 1, 1861, Lt. Charles Henry Tompkins, 2nd US Cavalry, led a raid on Fairfax Court House. After charging through lines of the Virginians twice, the Union cavalry was finally driven off. Tompkins received the Congressional Medal of Honor for his actions. In the morning, the body of Captain Marr of the Warrenton Rifles was discovered. Marr had been hit by a spent round ball. He had a large bruise above his heart but his skin had not been penetrated. Captain Marr's body arrived in Warrenton that evening, and he was buried the next afternoon after a ceremony in the clerk's office yard before a large crowd of mourners. (AC.)

On July 16, the Union army marched out of Washington to meet the Confederates at Manassas Junction. The Union troops marched through the sleepy village of Centreville, Virginia (seen here). On July 21, 1861, the two great armies grappled. Both sides had about 35,000 men. (LOC.)

The Union army was defeated on the plains of Manassas. The retreat was relatively orderly until the cry went up, "The Black Horse Cavalry are coming." At the Bull Run crossings (seen here), the retreat became a humiliating rout as soldiers streamed uncontrollably toward Centreville, discarding their arms and equipment. (LOC.)

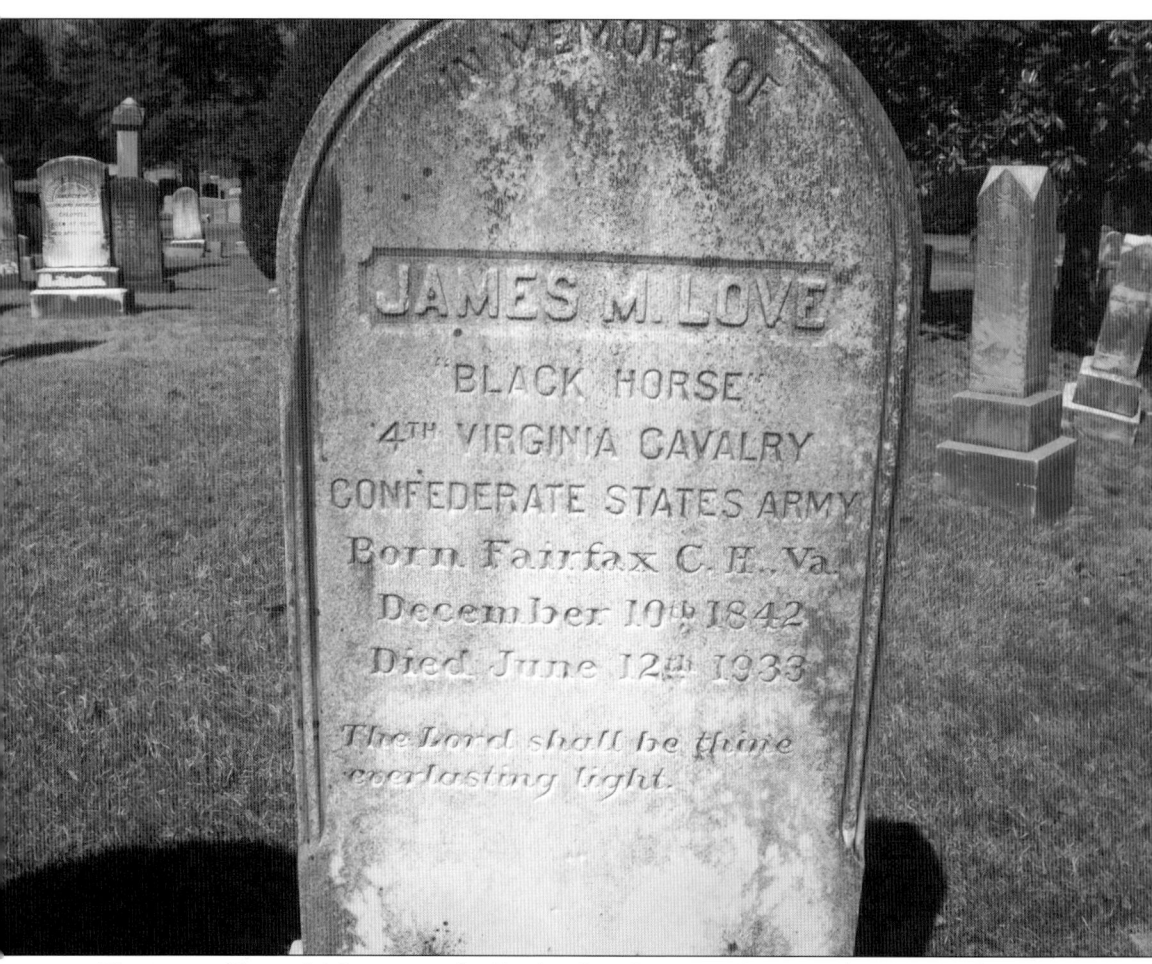

The grave of James M. Love is in the Fairfax City Cemetery. Love was born in Fairfax County in December 1842. He enlisted in the Black Horse troop, which became Company H of the 4th Virginia Cavalry. Love served as a private and participated in the celebrated raid around the Union army in 1862. In the spring of 1864, he was severely wounded, losing an arm. The Black Horse troop served in every major engagement in Virginia, from First Manassas to Appomattox Court House. They won a reputation as fierce fighters. In 1861, the *Richmond Inquirer* published this account of the Black Horse Cavalry in action: "the cavalry charged upon the regiment, hemming it in on all sides; and, cutting right and left with tremendous blows, each blow powerful enough to take off a man's head." (AC.)

Union major general Philip Kearny lost an arm in the Mexican-American War and commanded French troops in the Second Italian War of Independence. Kearny had the most combat experience of any general of either side at the start of the Civil War. He took command of the 1st New Jersey Brigade and trained it to be an efficient fighting force. At the Battle of Williamsburg, Kearny led a charge against Confederate troops with a sword in his one hand and the reins of his horse in his teeth. He was beloved and respected by common soldiers. In August 1862, General Kearny led his division at the Second Battle of Manassas, which saw the Union army routed and nearly destroyed. Kearny retreated toward Washington and fought the pursuing Confederates on September 1, 1862, at the Battle of Chantilly. The valiant Kearny was killed in action. (LOC.)

Philip Kearny (1815–1862) was killed in action at the Battle of Chantilly. Responding to warnings about his safety, he said, "The Rebel bullet that can kill me has not yet been molded." Encountering Confederate troops, Kearny refused a demand to surrender and was shot while trying to retreat. He died instantly. Confederate major general A.P. Hill said, "he deserved a better fate than to die in the mud." Kearny's body was sent to the Union line by Robert E. Lee under a flag of truce, and his death was mourned by officers on both sides. Kearny's body was embalmed and sent north for burial. Embalming methods advanced rapidly during the war. Dr. Thomas Holmes received a commission from the Army Medical Corps to embalm the corpses of dead Union officers to return to their families. Military authorities also permitted private embalmers to work in military-controlled areas. (LOC.)

Kearny was buried in New York. In 1912, his remains were exhumed and reinterred at Arlington National Cemetery (seen here). On April 7, 1912, the *Washington Post* reported, "Remains of Fighter Who Took Part in Four Wars, Won Daring Battle With Mexicans, and Was Slain in 1862, Will Be Buried With Full Military Honors: The body of Major General Phil Kearny, a hero of four wars, which for 50 years has lain in a grave in Trinity Cemetery, New York, will be buried in Arlington Cemetery on April 11 after full military services. The grave will be adjacent to that of General George A. Cook, a famous Indian fighter and hero of the Mexican war. An oration by 'Corpl.' James Tanner, register of wills for the District; prayers, and brief remarks by prominent army officers and music by the Fort Myer Band will constitute the program." (LOC.)

The reinterment drive was spearheaded by Charles F. Hopkins. In 1911, Hopkins led the drive to have his former brigade commander, Gen. Philip Kearny, disinterred from his unmarked grave in New York City's Trinity Churchyard and reburied with full military honors in Arlington National Cemetery. Hopkins was successful in his efforts, and General Kearny was reinterred in 1912 in a solemn military ceremony attended by many prominent Civil War veterans. A statue in Kearny's honor at Arlington National Cemetery is one of only two equestrian statues at Arlington. The statue was dedicated by Pres. Woodrow Wilson in November 1914 and was refurbished in 1996 by the New Jersey nonprofit General Philip Kearny Memorial Committee. When Hopkins died in 1934, he was the last remaining Civil War Medal of Honor recipient in New Jersey. (LOC.)

After the Second Battle of Manassas in August 1862, Clara Barton, a clerk at the Government Patent Office who had gathered a group of volunteers, nursed the wounded for three days at St. Mary's Church near Fairfax Station. Many soldiers died and were buried in the churchyard. As a result of her experiences in the Civil War, Barton went on to establish the American Red Cross. She began this project in 1873 but was initially told that since the United States would never again face a crisis like the Civil War, such an organization was unnecessary. Barton finally succeeded in convincing critics by using the argument that the new American Red Cross could respond to crises other than war, such as earthquakes, forest fires, and hurricanes. Clara Barton became president of the American Red Cross in May 1881. (LOC.)

In 1838, two Catholic families donated a tract of land in hopes of having a church built and a Catholic cemetery consecrated. A cemetery was created immediately. Irish immigrants became the nucleus of the new parish. Their names are inscribed on the cemetery's tombstones. St. Mary's Church (seen here) was dedicated in 1860. (AC.)

Union troops prepare to bury the dead. There was no official system for identifying the dead. The lucky could rely on friends to write to their family. In the spring of 1865, Clara Barton established the Missing Soldiers Office in Washington. This organization helped provide information about 22,000 soldiers to anxious families. (LOC.)

The Mount Vernon Ladies' Association took over operation of George Washington's estate at Mount Vernon in 1860 in an effort to stabilize and restore the mansion. As restoration efforts progressed, war broke out. Throughout the war, the estate was managed by two staff members, a northerner and a southerner. (LOC.)

Washington's tomb was a place of veneration for both Union and Confederate soldiers. Soldiers visiting the estate were requested to be neither armed nor dressed in military uniform. Such actions ensured that Mount Vernon remained neutral, hallowed ground. Mount Vernon remained safe and open throughout the war. (LOC.)

Pohick Church was the parish church of George Washington. During the Civil War, occupying Union forces stripped it for souvenirs of "Washington's Church." Lt. Charles B. Haydon, from Michigan, wrote, "I have long known that the Mich 2nd had no fear or reverence as a general thing for God or the places where he is worshiped." (LOC.)

Lieutenant Haydon continued, "They were all over it in less than 10 minutes tearing off the ornaments, splitting the woodwork and pews. . . . They wanted pieces to carry away. . . . A more absolute set of vandals than our men can not be found on the face of the earth." (LOC.)

A Confederate grave at Pohick Church is pictured here. A skirmish occurred here on August 18, 1861, when some 25 Union cavalrymen charged an equal number of Confederates. The Union cavalry pursued the retreating Confederates, but their officer reported that the enemy "were well mounted, had very superior horses, and were able to outfoot us." One Union soldier was killed. (AC.)

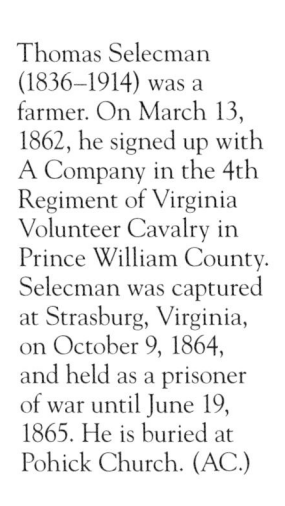

Thomas Selecman (1836–1914) was a farmer. On March 13, 1862, he signed up with A Company in the 4th Regiment of Virginia Volunteer Cavalry in Prince William County. Selecman was captured at Strasburg, Virginia, on October 9, 1864, and held as a prisoner of war until June 19, 1865. He is buried at Pohick Church. (AC.)

Alexander Chapman Williams (1837–1897) is buried at Pohick Church. Williams was a 24-year-old farmer when he enlisted in the Confederate army for 12 months' service in April 1861. The regimental muster roll described Chapman as "5'6", light complexion, gray hair, blue eyes." Williams served in the army for four years, reaching the rank of first lieutenant. (AC.)

The grave of Dr. Napoleon Bonaparte Nevitt (1831–1911) is at Pohick Church. Nevitt studied medicine at the University of Maryland and was a surgeon in the Confederate army throughout the Civil War. After the war, he had a private practice in Alexandria. Nevitt was a vestryman at Pohick Church for more than 40 years. (AC.)

The Falls Church, the church for which the city is named, was first built in 1734. The present-day brick church replaced the wooden one in 1769. By 1861, Falls Church had seen the arrival of many northerners seeking land. The township's vote for secession was about 75 percent for and 25 percent against. (LOC.)

The Falls Church was vandalized by occupying Union troops. The 83rd Pennsylvania Infantry, camped near Falls Church, confiscated fences and gates for firewood and even harvested five acres of potatoes. Volunteers of the 40th New York took pride in their nickname the "Forty Thieves," because they could find plunder where others failed. (LOC.)

There are currently two markers at the Falls Church, one for unknown Union soldiers and one for Confederate soldiers. These markers are located in the front of the churchyard on South Washington Street and were dedicated on Memorial Day 2004. The Union soldiers were from the 144th and 80th New York Volunteer Infantry Regiments, stationed at Upton's Hill. The soldiers all died of disease with the exception of one, who was "accidentally shot." The remains of a single unknown Confederate soldier were removed after the war. (Both, AC.)

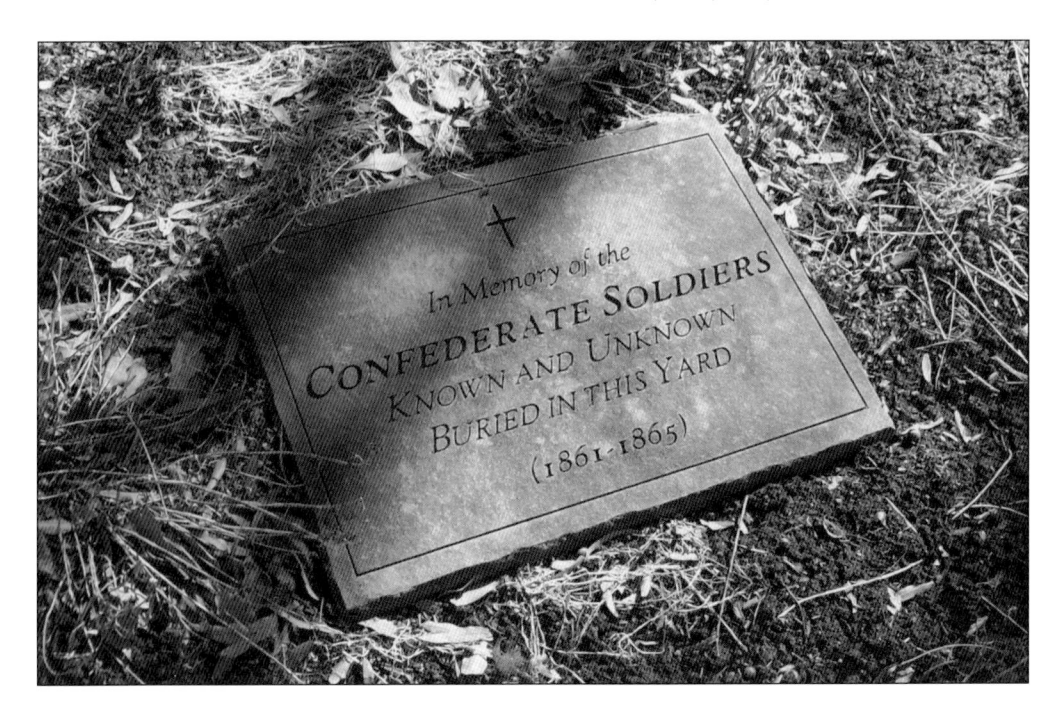

Fairfax City, then known as Fairfax Court House, was the scene of several notable events during the Civil War. Capt. John Quincy Marr, the first officer casualty of the Confederacy, was killed at Fairfax Court House on June 1, 1861. In March 1863, Union general Edwin H. Stoughton was captured in his bed by Confederate raider Col. John Singleton Mosby. Two historically priceless documents, the wills of George and Martha Washington, were housed in the Fairfax County Courthouse. When Union troops occupied the Fairfax area, the clerk of court instructed his wife to take George Washington's will to the home of their daughter near Warrenton, Virginia. In 1862, the will was taken to Richmond for safekeeping. Martha Washington's will remained at the Fairfax County Courthouse. In 1862, the courthouse was vandalized by Union troops, and Martha Washington's will was stolen. It was not returned until 1915. (LOC.)

During their occupation of the Fairfax Court House area in 1862–1863, Union troops occupied the estate at Blenheim and left graffiti throughout the house. The house contains one of the largest and best-preserved examples of Civil War inscriptions in the nation, a "diary on walls" providing insight into typical soldier life during the Civil War. (AC.)

The owner of Blenheim, Albert Willcoxon, supported the Confederate cause by selling supplies to the army. By October 1862, Fairfax County was firmly in Union hands. Willcoxon, his wife, and their two children fled the area. The family cemetery, located next to the house, includes four generations of the Willcoxon family. (AC.)

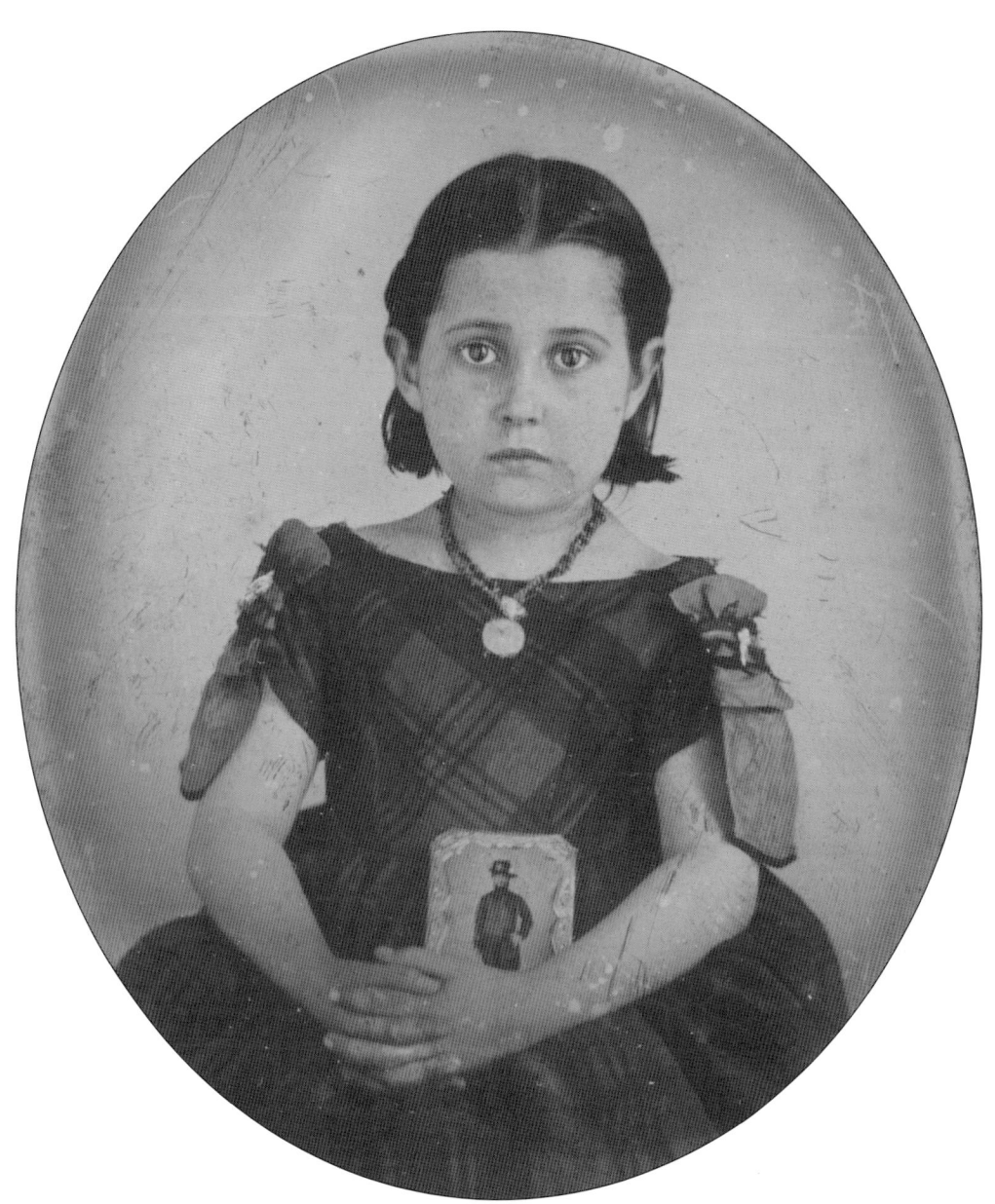

During the four years of the Civil War, 26 major battles and 400 smaller engagements were fought in Virginia. Few stop to think about the impact these battles had on civilians. Here a young girl, dressed in mourning, holds a picture of her dead father, dressed in uniform. In the 1860s, America was a profoundly religious nation. People expected to die at home surrounded by family and friends in the hope that they would all be reunited in heaven. Most soldiers died alone, unknown, and without comfort, their families in total ignorance of their fate. After the war, the rhythms of life reasserted themselves. The Blue Ridge Mountains rose high and blue in the west. At sunset, it seemed as if the world ended at the mountains. Small children closed their eyes and listened to their mothers sing, "Beyond the sunset's radiant glow, there is a brighter world, I know." (LOC.)

Union dead are buried at Langley. Thirteen regiments of Pennsylvania volunteers, styled the "Pennsylvania Reserves," crossed the Potomac River on the Chain Bridge and entered Virginia on October 9, 1861. They set up camp near Langley in the area of the current-day intersection of the Georgetown Pike and Balls Hill Road. (LOC.)

At the end of the war in April 1865, tens of thousands of soldiers still lay unburied, their bones littering battlefields. Many more had been hastily buried where they fell, often in mass graves. Congress appropriated money to reinter Union soldiers in national cemeteries, but the Confederate dead were abandoned by the federal government. (LOC.)

In 1866, the trustees of the Ladies' Memorial Association canvassed the county, and eventually some 200 unknown Confederate soldiers were reburied in a common grave atop the hill in the Fairfax City Cemetery. In 1875, ownership of the cemetery was conveyed to the trustees of the newly chartered Fairfax Cemetery Association. (AC.)

In 1888, the Confederate Monument Association was formed to erect a suitable monument to both the unknown Confederate dead buried in the cemetery and the Confederate soldiers from Fairfax who lay on battlefields far from home. In October 1890, the monument was officially dedicated. Control of the cemetery passed to the City of Fairfax in 1962. (AC.)

The Confederate monument at the Fairfax City Cemetery was erected to "the memory of the gallant sons of Fairfax, whose names are inscribed on this monument but whose bodies lie buried on distant battlefields, and to the memory of their 200 unknown comrades whose remains are at rest beneath this mound." (AC.)

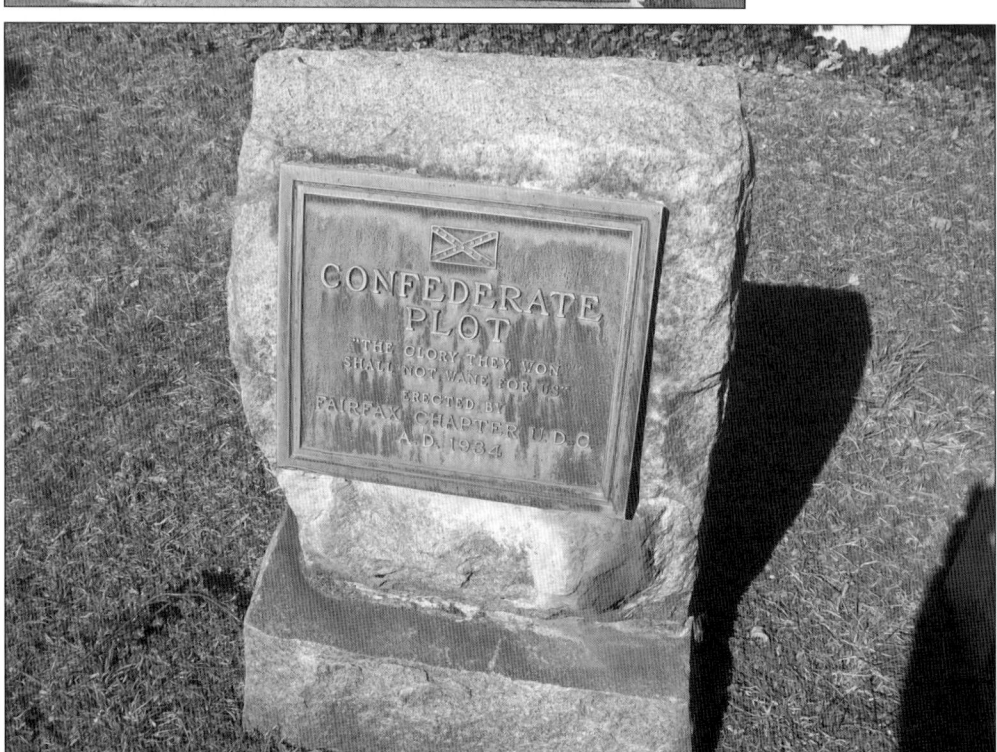

A memorial was placed at the Fairfax City Cemetery by the United Daughters of the Confederacy (UDC). Founded in 1894, the UDC was influential throughout the South in preserving and upholding the memory of Confederate veterans, especially those husbands, sons, fathers, and brothers who died in the war. The UDC still exists. (AC.)

The Southern Cross of Honor (seen in front of this grave) was created by the United Daughters of the Confederacy and is used as a symbol on the graves of Confederate veterans in recognition of "loyal, honorable service." The Southern Cross takes two different forms. One is an engraved outline on the gravestone. The other is a two-sided, cast iron replica of the medal placed at the grave site. (AC.)

The Jermantown Cemetery was established in 1868 for African American residents who could not be buried in the segregated Fairfax City Cemetery. There are over 40 headstones and an undetermined number of unmarked graves. Since there are no more trustees to care for the cemetery, Fairfax City has maintained the mowing of the cemetery. (AC.)

Notable among those buried in the Jermantown Cemetery is George Lamb, a free African American who served in the Confederate army as a body servant to Capt. William H. Dulany of the Fairfax Rifles. Lamb remained with the 17th Virginia throughout the war, even after Dulany was severely wounded at Blackburn's Ford in 1861. What motivated the 27-year-old Lamb to remain with the Fairfax Rifles is unknown. After the Civil War, Lamb worked as a blacksmith for Joseph Cooper, who ran a wagon shop in Fairfax. Lamb never married and died of influenza in 1926 at the age of 92. His epitaph reads, "He was loyal and true to his friends." Lamb was described as being five feet, eight inches tall, with black eyes, a full face, and no perceivable marks or scars. (AC.)

Flint Hill Cemetery is the resting place of a number of Civil War–era military and civilian figures. Twenty-four veterans, including four who served in Confederate colonel John S. Mosby's partisan rangers, are buried here. The first documented burial here occurred in 1852, when present-day Oakton was called Flint Hill. (AC.)

Josiah B. Bowman (1827–1904), who owned Ayr Hill in Vienna and served as one of Union spymaster Col. Lafayette C. Baker's agents, is buried at Flint Hill. Flint Hill is the final resting place of two other Union soldiers, Pvt. Isaac F. Jenkins and Pvt. Jacob Snowden, Company I, 105th Pennsylvania Infantry. (AC.)

The grave of Robert G. Clarke (1841–1918) is pictured at Flint Hill Cemetery. Clarke enlisted as a private in the 30th Virginia Infantry. He was wounded on May 16, 1864, near Drewry's Bluff, Virginia. His second wife, Mary Adelaid Dishman Clarke, the sister of his first wife, Julia Augusta Dishman Clarke, is buried next to him. (AC.)

The dead await burial. There was limited ability to preserve bodies for proper burial at home. As the practice of embalming became more widespread, embalmers followed the troops to the battlefront. After a battle, embalmers would seek out dead officers, knowing they could command high fees from the family of the officer. (LOC.)

Civil War burials are still being found as new developments are built. In 1997, a relic hunter stumbled on a Civil War burial site in the Centreville area on property scheduled to be developed for a fast-food restaurant. While exploring a field near 5900 Centreville Road (Route 28, seen here), relic hunter Kevin Ambrose discovered a human skull and contacted county archaeologists, who determined that six soldiers were buried at the site. Because they were buried in coffins and not in a mass grave, archaeologists believe that the soldiers died of disease. Many objects were excavated at the site, including pieces of clothing, brass-embossed buttons, white milk-glass buttons, suspender buckles, shoes, minié balls, canvas boots, and the remnants of wooden coffins. The military buttons indicate that the soldiers were probably buried in the first year of the war and that the men were Union soldiers. (LOC.)

A Confederate cemetery has been reported in the heavily wooded Union Mills area near Clifton. The site is said to be on the north side of the Southern Railway tracks. Union Mills Station was among the first stations opened when the Orange & Alexandria Railroad began operation in the early 1850s. During the first year of the war, the Confederates made the Union Mills area part of the defense line that ran across Northern Virginia. After the Confederates departed in early 1862, Union troops were stationed at Union Mills to protect the railroad bridge from Confederate raiders. The bridge was destroyed and rebuilt seven times during the war. The modern railroad follows the route of the old Orange & Alexandria line. The abutments of the Civil War–era bridge still stand next to the current railroad bridge over Bull Run. (LOC.)

Four

Mosby's Confederacy

Because most of the fighting during the Civil War occurred in the South, the Confederacy often resorted to unorthodox methods in fighting the war. One expedient was the organization of bands of armed irregulars who were given license to carry out guerilla warfare behind enemy lines. On April 21, 1862, the Confederate Congress authorized the formation of "partisan rangers." Native to the area and intimately familiar with every hill and stream, the partisan rangers staged daring hit-and-run attacks against vastly superior Union forces. Fed and shielded by sympathetic locals, the guerillas were a major irritant to the Union army.

North central Virginia became the preserve of one of the most dashing figures of the war, John Singleton Mosby. Mosby grew up in the shadow of the central Blue Ridge, attended the University of Virginia, and practiced law in southwest Virginia. He signed up for Confederate service shortly after the firing at Fort Sumter. By the summer of 1861, he was part of Stuart's cavalry. He served as Stuart's scout throughout much of 1862 and accompanied him on his Fairfax raid in December of that year. When Stuart rode out of Fairfax County, Mosby, with nine men, had permission to remain behind.

Northern Virginia was a region of small and scattered communities set amid gently rolling hills. It was an ideal area for cavalry operations; in the last three years of the war, Mosby's horsemen so dominated activities in the area that it was often called "Mosby's Confederacy." Mosby was everywhere. He destroyed railway tracks and robbed sutlers and Union paymasters. He captured pickets and shot down stragglers. With a price on his head, he crossed Long Bridge into Washington in the full light of day. There, he hobnobbed with Union officers at the bar of the Willard Hotel, and returned unharmed to Virginia. On one occasion, Mosby stopped ladies on their way to Washington and sent a lock of his hair to President Lincoln, accompanied by a note expressing regret that he could not deliver it himself.

North central Virginia became the preserve of one of the most dashing figures of the war, John Singleton Mosby (1833–1916), nicknamed the "Gray Ghost." Mosby commanded the 43rd Battalion, 1st Virginia Cavalry, known to history as "Mosby's Rangers" or "Mosby's Raiders." The 43rd Battalion operated officially as a unit of the Army of Northern Virginia, but the 1,900 men who served under Mosby from January 1863 through April 1865 lived outside of the norms of the regular army. The Confederate government created special rules to govern partisan rangers such as Mosby's men. These rules included permission to share in the disposition of the spoils of war. Because of this, Union officers considered Mosby's men little better than common outlaws. In 1864, several of Mosby's men captured in battle were executed by Union forces. Mosby retaliated, executing a similar number of Union soldiers. (LOC.)

Mosby's men immobilized 30,000 Union troops. Mosby's command, often consisting of fewer than 50 men, captured thousands of Union troops, horses, and mules. Soon civilians in the area became conscious of the Mosby magic and offered to enlist under the Confederate law that authorized the creation of guerilla bands. (LOC.)

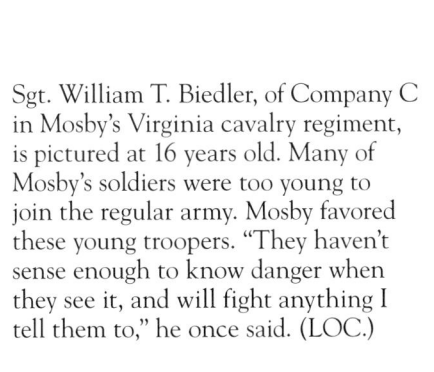

Sgt. William T. Biedler, of Company C in Mosby's Virginia cavalry regiment, is pictured at 16 years old. Many of Mosby's soldiers were too young to join the regular army. Mosby favored these young troopers. "They haven't sense enough to know danger when they see it, and will fight anything I tell them to," he once said. (LOC.)

The village of Fairfax Court House is where Mosby captured Union general Edwin H. Stoughton. Mosby found Stoughton asleep in bed. Awakening the general with a slap to the rear, Mosby asked "Do you know Mosby, General?" The general replied "Yes! Have you caught him?" "No," said Mosby. "But, he's caught you!" (LOC.)

Mosby's command, the 43rd Battalion, 1st Virginia Cavalry, was known for lightning-quick raids and a remarkable ability to elude the Union army. Some 2,000 men served with Mosby during the war. The graves of Mosby's Raiders can be found in many area cemeteries, such as this one in Greenwich in Prince William County. (AC.)

A poignant reminder of the Civil War is the gravestone of Bradford Smiths Hoskins at Greenwich. Hopkins, "Late Capt. in her Britannic Majesty's Forty Fourth Regiment," according to his gravestone, was a British officer fighting under the command of Colonel Mosby. It was not unusual to find British officers visiting or even fighting with the opposing armies. (AC.)

Mosby opened a law practice in Warrenton after the war. For nine years, he lived in the large white house at 173 Main Street. When he decided to support President Grant and the Republican Party, many called him a turncoat. One night, someone shot at Mosby after he disembarked from a train at the depot. (LOC.)

Mosby disapproved of slavery but once said, "I am not ashamed of having fought on the side of slavery—a soldier fights for his country—right or wrong—he is not responsible for the political merits of the course he fights in. . . . The South was my country." (LOC.)

Mosby veterans are seen here at a reunion. Mosby never officially surrendered to Federal forces. He wrote of his exploits, "It is a classical maxim that it is sweet and becoming to die for one's country; but whoever has seen the horrors of a battlefield feels that it is far sweeter to live for it." (LOC.)

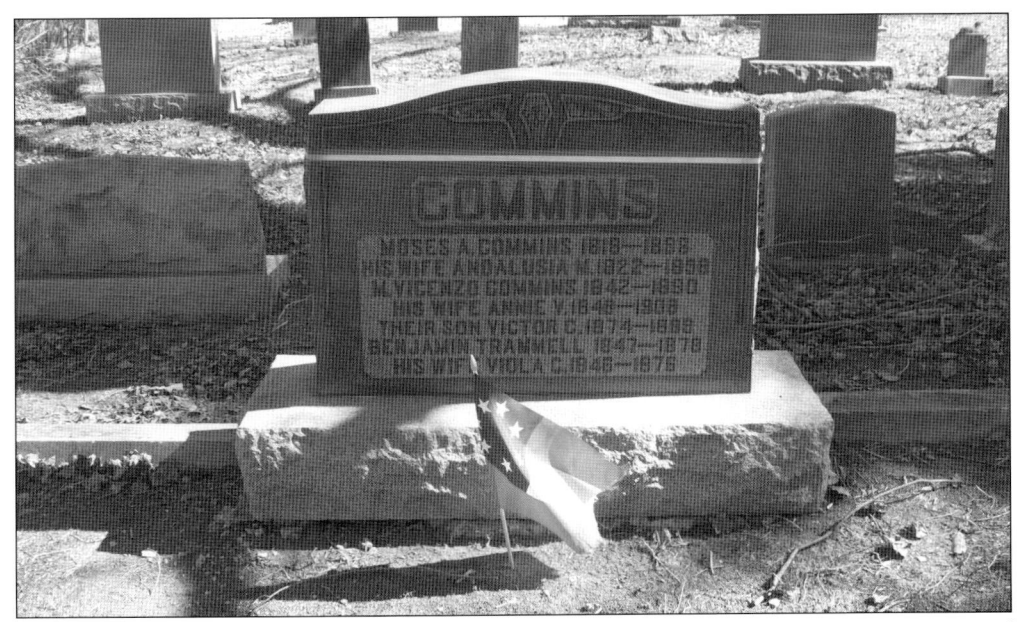

Four of Mosby's Rangers are buried at Flint Hill Cemetery in Fairfax County. Sam Moore of Berryville in Loudon County wrote, "They had for us all the glamour of Robin Hood and his merry men, all the courage and bravery of the ancient crusaders, the unexpectedness of benevolent pirates and the stealth of Indians." (AC.)

The Confederate monument at the Fairfax City Cemetery notes residents of Fairfax County who served with Mosby's cavalry. A few of Mosby's men were in their 40s, but most were in their late teens or early 20s; two young troopers paroled near the end of the war were only 14 years old. (AC.)

Mosby's grave is at the Warrenton Cemetery. As a child, Mosby was small, sickly, and often the target of bullying. He would respond by fighting back. During the course of the war, Mosby was wounded seven times. For someone who had been a sickly youth, he proved quite resilient, dying at the age of 82 on May 30, 1916. Sixty-six of Mosby's Rangers are buried in the same cemetery. After the war, the 31-year-old Mosby went on to become a distinguished railway lawyer. He also served as US consul to Hong Kong and in several other federal government posts. Although Mosby's wartime exploits have been romanticized, he himself once said that there was "no man in the Confederate army who had less of the spirit of knight-errantry in him, or took a more practical view of war than I did." (AC.)

Five

Arlington National Cemetery

Arlington National Cemetery was created as a Union military cemetery on an estate called Arlington House, which was owned by Mary Custis Lee, the wife of Confederate general Robert E. Lee. The first official military burial occurred in 1864. By the end of the Civil War, in April 1865, there were some 16,000 burials at Arlington.

Neither Robert E. Lee nor his wife ever set foot in Arlington House after the war. General Lee died on October 12, 1870, in Lexington, Virginia. Mary Custis Lee visited the grounds shortly before her death in 1873, but was overcome by emotion and was unable to go inside the house. After the death of his parents, George Washington Custis Lee claimed that the house and land had been illegally confiscated during the Civil War and that, according to his grandfather's will, he was the legal owner of the property. In December 1882, the US Supreme Court, in a 5-4 decision, returned the property to George Washington Custis Lee, stating that it had been confiscated without due process. Would the dead have to be transferred to a new site? General Lee's son diffused the crisis by selling the house and land to the government for its fair market value.

In 1920, Alexandria County was renamed Arlington County to honor Robert E. Lee and to end the ongoing confusion between Alexandria County and the independent city of Alexandria. Arlington House itself was subsequently dedicated to the memory of Robert E. Lee.

Today, Arlington National Cemetery encompasses 624 acres and is divided into 70 sections, including the Confederate Section, the section for those who died in the Global War on Terror, and the Nurses Section. The remains of more than 400,000 people from the United States and 11 other countries are buried at Arlington, including some 400 Medal of Honor recipients. Four million people visit the cemetery annually.

There are 28 major and 142 minor monuments and memorials within the cemetery's grounds. The first major memorial was completed in 1866. The original entry gates to the cemetery were later dedicated to Union generals.

George Washington Parke Custis inherited 1,100 acres overlooking the Potomac River, when his father, the stepson of Gen. George Washington, died. Upon reaching legal age in 1802, the young man began building a lavish house that was to be not only his house but also a living memorial to George Washington. (LOC.)

Originally the name "Mount Washington" was considered for the house, but in the end it was named after the Custis family estate in the Virginia Tidewater area and became known as Arlington House. George Washington Parke Custis died in 1857 and was buried on the estate. His grave is seen here. (AC.)

Custis married and had one daughter, Mary. Mary Custis, one of the wealthiest heiresses in Virginia, fell in love with a penniless soldier, Robert E. Lee. Although Lee came from a prominent family, at the time of his birth, there was no family fortune left. Lee had only his army pay and his person to offer a bride. (LOC.)

Under the terms of her father's will, Mary Lee was allowed to live in and control Arlington House during her lifetime, at which point the house would pass to her eldest son. Mary and Robert E. Lee lived in Arlington House until 1861, when Lee went south to join the Confederate army. (LOC.)

Union troops moved into Virginia in May 1861, immediately taking up positions around Arlington House. Two forts were built on the estate: Fort Whipple (now Fort Myer) and Fort McPherson. The property was confiscated by the federal government when property taxes were not paid in person by Mary Lee. (LOC.)

The property was offered for public sale on January 11, 1864, and was purchased by a tax commissioner for "government use, for war, military, charitable and educational purposes." Union officers are seen here on the front porch of Arlington House. Neither Robert E. Lee nor his wife ever set foot in Arlington House again. (LOC.)

Brig. Gen. Montgomery C. Meigs, commander of the garrison at Arlington House and quartermaster general of the Union army, who may have had a grudge against Robert E. Lee, was tasked with finding additional burial grounds for battle casualties. Meigs and Lee had served together many years earlier as military engineers on the Mississippi River. Lee was a first lieutenant and Meigs, a second lieutenant, was his subordinate. Did Meigs bear Lee a personal grudge? Some historians think so, or perhaps he was just embittered by the war itself or by Lee's defection from the Union army. Meigs wrote to the secretary of war stating that "the grounds about the mansion are admirably suited to such a use." Meigs reported his "grim satisfaction" of ordering 26 Union dead to be buried near Mary Lee's rose garden in June 1864. (LOC.)

Private William Henry Christman from Pennsylvania was the first soldier to be officially buried at Arlington. A laborer, Christman enlisted on March 25, 1864. He was hospitalized for measles five weeks later and died on May 11. He was buried on May 13, 1864. (AC.)

Montgomery Meigs's own son was killed in October 1864 and is buried at Arlington Cemetery. The funeral of John Rodgers Meigs was attended by President Lincoln and other dignitaries. He was eulogized by Secretary of War Edwin M. Stanton as "One of the youngest and brightest of the military profession, he has fallen an early victim to murderous rebel warfare." (AC.)

John Rodgers Meigs's tomb is covered by a bronze sculpture of Meigs two-thirds life-size in the uniform of a first lieutenant of engineers, lying on his back in the mud. The hooves of horses ridden by Confederate cavalrymen have trampled on the body and left imprints in the mud. (AC.)

The Civil War Unknowns Monument was the inspiration for Montgomery Meigs's own tomb, also located at Arlington National Cemetery. Meigs erected the sarcophagus over the grave of his wife, and he himself was buried there in 1892. The lid was modeled after the Ark of the Covenant described in the book of Exodus. (AC.)

97

Hay barns and barracks surround Arlington House. The large number of impoverished freed slaves created a problem. In May 1863, the military recommended their resettlement in the "pure country area" of Robert E. Lee's Arlington estate in Alexandria County. Freedman's Village, Arlington, one of many throughout the United States, was formally opened on December 4, 1863. (LOC.)

The southern portion of the land now occupied by the cemetery was used during and after the Civil War as a settlement for freed slaves. More than 1,100 freed slaves were given land by the government at Freedman's Village (seen here), where they farmed and lived during and after the Civil War. They were evicted in 1888. (LOC.)

Arlington National Cemetery was segregated until 1948. Veterans of the US Colored Troops (USCT) were buried in Section 27. The 175 regiments of the USCT made up some 10 percent of the Union army. The unit seen here was stationed near Arlington. After the Civil War, soldiers in the USCT fought in the Indian Wars in the American West. Frederick Douglass, the most prominent African American intellectual of the Civil War era, wrote, "[He] who would be free must himself strike the blow." The USCT was the answer to that call. Some 40,000 gave their lives for the cause. Douglass wrote, "Once let the black man get upon his person the brass letters U.S.; let him get an eagle on his button, and a musket on his shoulder, and bullets in his pocket, and there is no power on the earth or under the earth which can deny that he has earned the right of citizenship in the United States." (LOC.)

Freedman's Village was intended to be a temporary refuge where ex-slaves would receive a basic education and be taught vocations before leaving to find work elsewhere. The population of the village boomed and residents settled into the community. The village turned into a semi-permanent settlement. Freed men who did not have work elsewhere worked on the government-owned farms that surrounded the village at Arlington. African American laborers were paid $10 per month. The workers paid half of this back to the government in rent for the maintenance of the village. More than 3,800 former slaves, called "contrabands" during the Civil War, are buried in Section 27. Their headstones are designated with the word "Civilian" or "Citizen." (LOC.)

BENEATH THIS STONE
REPOSE THE BONES OF TWO THOUSAND ONE HUNDRED AND ELEVEN UNKNOWN SOLDIERS
GATHERED AFTER THE WAR
FROM THE FIELDS OF BULL RUN, AND THE ROUTE TO THE RAPPAHANNOCK.
THEIR REMAINS COULD NOT BE IDENTIFIED, BUT THEIR NAMES AND DEATHS ARE
RECORDED IN THE ARCHIVES OF THEIR COUNTRY; AND ITS GRATEFUL CITIZENS
HONOR THEM AS OF THEIR NOBLE ARMY OF MARTYRS. MAY THEY REST IN PEACE!
SEPTEMBER, A.D. 1866.

The first memorial constructed at Arlington was the Civil War Unknowns Monument, which was meant as a tribute to Union soldiers. Bodies of 2,111 dead soldiers were collected within a 35-mile radius. Most were full or partial remains discovered unburied and unidentifiable. The inscription on the west face of the memorial is visible here. This site was once a grove of trees near one of the estate's flower gardens. (LOC.)

Originally, a Rodman gun was placed at each corner, and a pyramid of shot adorned the center of the lid. By 1893, the memorial had been redesigned. The plain walls had been embellished, and although the inscription had been retained, the lid was replaced by one modeled after the Ark of the Covenant. (LOC.)

Several hundred Confederate dead were buried at Arlington by the end of the war in April 1865. Some were prisoners of war who died in custody. Some were executed spies. Some, because of the inability to identify remains, were probably buried in the monument to the Union dead. (LOC.)

In 1868, families of dead Confederates were barred from the cemetery on Decoration Day (now Memorial Day). Union veterans prowled the cemetery ensuring that Confederate graves were not honored in any way. Families of Confederates buried at Arlington were refused permission to lay flowers on their loved ones' graves. (LOC.)

Because of the Spanish-American War, the federal government's policy toward Confederate graves at Arlington National Cemetery changed. On December 14, 1898, President McKinley announced that the federal government would begin tending Confederate graves since these dead represented "a tribute to American valor." On June 4, 1914, Pres. Woodrow Wilson dedicated the Confederate Memorial at Arlington. (LOC.)

Construction of the Confederate Memorial (seen here) was initially opposed by some Southern organizations that regarded accepting an offer of a Confederate section at Arlington as a sign of accommodation with the United States, arguing that Confederate dead should lie in Southern soil. In 1901, several Confederate veterans' groups convinced all sides to proceed. (LOC.)

Several hundred Confederate were disinterred and reburied in a Confederate section around the spot designated for the Confederate Memorial. The Confederate Memorial was dedicated to reconciliation and the hope of a united future. US presidents have traditionally sent a wreath to be placed at the Confederate Memorial on Memorial Day. (LOC.)

A competition was held to select the sculptor of the Confederate Memorial at Arlington National Cemetery. Moses Ezekiel won the competition and entitled his work *The New South*. The monument's focus is on peace, the future, and the sacrifices made by the common soldier. The Confederate Monument was unveiled on June 4, 1914. Pres. Woodrow Wilson delivered an address, and both Union and Confederate veterans honored their former foes, symbolizing the reconciliation between the North and South, the memorial's central theme. Some 482 people are buried in the Confederate section, including 46 officers, 351 enlisted men, 58 wives, 15 civilians, and 12 unknowns. The dead are buried in concentric circles around the Confederate Monument, and their graves are marked with headstones that are distinct for their pointed tops. Moses Ezekiel is buried at the base of the famous monument he created. (LOC.)

One of the notables buried at Arlington is Philip H. Sheridan (1831–1888), who led the Cavalry Corps of the Army of the Potomac during the Civil War. In 1865, his cavalry was instrumental in forcing the Confederate surrender at Appomattox. Sheridan later fought Indians during the Plains Wars. (LOC.)

Sheridan was promoted to lieutenant general in 1884 and took command of the US Army. In 1888, he was promoted to general. He finished writing the *Personal Memoirs of P.H. Sheridan* just before he died on August 5, 1888. (LOC.)

One of the earliest memorials built in the cemetery was the Sheridan Gate. The gate was built in 1879 as one of the entrances to the then walled cemetery and was dedicated to Sheridan after his death. The columns were originally erected in the portico of the old War Department building in Washington, DC. After that building was demolished in 1879, the columns were moved to Arlington. By the mid-1900s, the gate was no longer able to accommodate the trucks and construction equipment that were vital to the cemetery's expansion. In 1971, the cemetery expanded, and the Sheridan Gate was dismantled. Arlington National Cemetery is working with a Seattle-based team of forensic and preservation experts and the US Army Corps of Engineers to assess the condition and restore the historic stone columns that were once used for the Sheridan and Ord-Weitzel Gates. (LOC.)

Maj. Gen. Edward O.C. Ord is pictured with his family. Ord's career peaked in 1865, when he led a forced march to Appomattox Court House and forced the surrender of Robert E. Lee's Confederate army. Gen. William T. Sherman said that Ord's "skillful, hard march the night before was one of the chief causes of Lee's surrender." (LOC.)

One of the earliest memorials was the Ord-Weitzel Gate, completed in 1879. This gate was initially unnamed. In 1902, with the deaths of two prominent Union generals, Edward O.C. Ord and Godfrey Weitzel, the gate was dedicated as the Ord-Weitzel Gate. The gate was dismantled in 1971 at the time of the cemetery's expansion. (LOC.)

Maj. Gen. George B. McClellan, seen here with his wife, was a controversial military officer during the early part of the war. Accused of "having the slows" by President Lincoln, McClellan was a brilliant administrative officer but timid on the battlefield. McClellan ran against Lincoln in the presidential election of 1864. (LOC.)

In 1867, Congress required that all military cemeteries be fenced. A red Seneca sandstone wall was built around Arlington Cemetery. The original main gate of the cemetery was dedicated to Maj. Gen. George B. McClellan and is seen here. The McClellan Gate was completed in 1879. (AC.)

Joseph "Fighting Joe" Wheeler (1836–1906) served as general in the Confederate army in the 1860s and as a general in the US Army during the Spanish-American War in 1898. In 1898, Wheeler commanded the cavalry division that included Teddy Roosevelt's famous "Rough Riders." The bearded Wheeler is seen here with Roosevelt and others. (LOC.)

The grave of Joseph Wheeler is pictured here. One of Wheeler's former Confederate comrades in arms, James Longstreet, said upon seeing Wheeler in a US Army uniform, "Joe, I hope that Almighty God takes me before he does you, for I want to be within the gates of hell to hear Jubal Early cuss you in the blue uniform." (LOC.)

Another of the notables buried at Arlington is Abner Doubleday (1819–1893). Doubleday was a career soldier. He fired the first shot in defense of Fort Sumter. He also played a pivotal part at the Battle of Gettysburg. He is best remembered as the inventor of baseball, an honor that some contest. (LOC.)

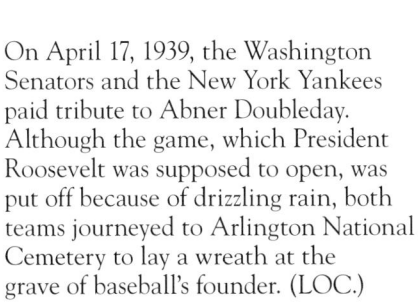

On April 17, 1939, the Washington Senators and the New York Yankees paid tribute to Abner Doubleday. Although the game, which President Roosevelt was supposed to open, was put off because of drizzling rain, both teams journeyed to Arlington National Cemetery to lay a wreath at the grave of baseball's founder. (LOC.)

111

The legend of George Armstrong Custer began at the First Battle of Manassas. Custer would enjoy a spectacularly successful military career until massacred by Sioux Indians in 1876 at the Battle of the Little Bighorn. Custer is buried at West Point, but some of those involved in his legend are buried at Arlington. Since his death along the bluffs overlooking the Little Bighorn River in Montana on June 25, 1876, over 500 books have been written about his life and career. Views of Custer have changed over succeeding generations. He has been portrayed as a callous egotist, a bungling egomaniac, a genocidal war criminal, and the puppet of faceless forces. Whatever else Custer may or may not have been, even in the 21st century, he remains the great lightning rod of American history. (LOC.)

William W. Belknap was a brigadier general for the Union during the Civil War and served as secretary of war during the Grant administration. By 1875, allegations of bribery surrounded Belknap because of his appointment of post traders who sold merchandise on military installations. George Armstrong Custer was called to testify before Congress in the matter. (LOC.)

Pictured is the grave of William Belknap. Custer accused President Grant's brother and Secretary of War Belknap of corruption. Belknap was impeached and sent to the Senate for trial. President Grant stripped Custer of overall command of the column chosen to subdue the Sioux and placed him under the command of Brig. Gen. Alfred Terry. Custer lost his life trying to regain his career. (AC.)

This is the grave of Frederick Benteen (1834–1898). A brevet colonel in the Civil War, Benteen served under Custer at the Battle of the Little Bighorn. Some blame Benteen for not coming to Custer's aid quickly enough, while others claim he did all he could and that his leadership saved a significant portion of the regiment from being massacred with Custer. Many officers admired Benteen for his fearlessness in battle. Benteen explained his actions at the Battle of the Little Bighorn to an 1879 court of inquiry: "We were at their hearths and homes, their medicine was working well, and they were fighting for all the good God gives anyone to fight for." Benteen was never found guilty of wrongdoing or dereliction of duty for his actions in the battle. He was brevetted brigadier general in 1890 after an active and tumultuous career. (AC.)

Six

OTHER NOTABLE GRAVES

The war began auspiciously for the Confederacy. In addition to victory at the First Battle of Manassas in July 1861, the Confederates won a small but stunning victory at the Battle of Ball's Bluff in Loudon County. On October 21, 1861, victorious Confederates drove Union troops over the bluff and into the Potomac River, where many drowned and hundreds surrendered. A sitting US senator, Col. Edward Baker, was killed. Bodies of dead Union soldiers floated down the river and washed up in Washington.

Despite early Confederate victories on the very doorstep of the nation's capital, the North persevered for four long bloody years, finally achieving total victory. During these four years, many military reputations were made and lost on the battlefields of Virginia. Among those who played a prominent part in shaping the history of Northern Virginia were Robert E. Lee, Thomas J. Jackson, and J.E.B. Stuart, all buried in Virginia.

By 1865, after 26 major battles and 300 smaller engagements on its soil, Virginia lay prostrate. As a percentage of national population, deaths in the Civil War would equate to some seven million people today. The generation of Americans that survived the Civil War lived the rest of their lives with grief and loss. Almost everyone knew someone who had been killed or wounded during the war. Many never got over the deaths of loved ones and lived in perpetual mourning. The nation took decades to even begin the healing process.

After the war, Union and Confederate veterans formed fraternal groups. These groups were often instrumental in speeding national reconciliation. In July 1911, the town of Manassas hosted a peace jubilee. George Carr Round, a Union veteran who settled in Manassas, is credited with this gesture of reconciliation. At noon on July 21, the 50th anniversary of the First Battle of Manassas, the Union and Confederate veterans moved to the top of Henry Hill. When the signal was given, the veterans marched forward with hands outstretched. For five minutes, they shook hands on the same field where they had once tried to kill one another.

In October, 1861, Union forces tried to cross the Potomac River near Leesburg and were disastrously repulsed on the steep cliffs at Ball's Bluff. Many fleeing Union soldiers were forced into the Potomac River, where they drowned. Bodies of Union soldiers floated down the Potomac and washed up in Washington, impacting Northern morale. (LOC.)

Most of the fallen Union soldiers found on or near the battlefield were buried in shallow mass graves. In 1865, Gov. Andrew Curtin of Pennsylvania tried to have his state's dead returned home. Four years after the war, however, individual remains could not be identified, so the US Army decided to establish a cemetery at Ball's Bluff for the Union dead. (LOC.)

Pictured is the cemetery gate at Ball's Bluff. The Union defeat caused members of Congress to suspect that there was a conspiracy to betray the Union. Defeats at Manassas (Bull Run), Wilson's Creek, and Ball's Bluff led to the establishment of the Congressional Joint Committee on the Conduct of the War, which would plague the military for the remainder of the war. (AC.)

Twenty-five graves in one of America's smallest national cemeteries contain the partial remains of 54 Union soldiers killed at the Battle of Ball's Bluff on October 21, 1861. All are unidentified Union soldiers except Pvt. James Allen of Northbridge, Massachusetts, who served with the 15th Massachusetts Infantry. (AC.)

Edward Dickinson Baker (1811–1861) served in the US House of Representatives from Illinois and later as a US Senator from Oregon. He was a longtime friend of President Lincoln. Baker served during both the Mexican-American War and the Civil War. On October 21, at the Battle of Ball's Bluff, he was struck by a volley of bullets that killed him instantly. Lincoln cried when he received the news of Baker's death. At Baker's funeral, Mary Todd Lincoln scandalized Washington by appearing in lilac rather than the traditional black. Col. Edward D. Baker is buried in San Francisco. This memorial stone was placed at Ball's Bluff to mark the spot of Baker's death and to honor the memory of the only sitting US senator to have ever died on the field of battle. Baker once said, "The officer who dies with his men will never be harshly judged." (AC.)

The Jackson statue at the Manassas battlefield is pictured here. On July 21, 1861, the 7th Georgia and 4th Alabama Regiments were badly cut up. Brig. Gen. Barnard Bee was compelled to give the order to fall back. Attempting to rally the retreating men, Bee used Gen. Thomas J. Jackson's newly arrived brigade as an anchor. Pointing to Jackson, Bee shouted, "There stands Jackson like a stone wall! Rally behind the Virginians!" Jackson was a tough fighter but also very religious. He exhorted one officer to "pray without ceasing." Jackson insisted that it could easily be done. "When we take our meals there is grace. When I take a draught of water I always pause, as my palate receives the refreshment, to lift up my heart to God. . . . And so of every other familiar act of the day." Many officers and men, impressed by Jackson's general religious character, said, "If that is religion, I must have it." (LOC.)

Gen. Thomas J. Jackson died after being accidentally wounded by one of his own men at the Battle of Chancellorsville in 1863. At the time of his death, a chaplain was close at hand, his wife sang hymns, and he exhibited a peaceful air. "Stonewall" Jackson attained mythological standing in Southern culture. (LOC.)

A statue of Confederate general Thomas "Stonewall" Jackson stands in the Stonewall Jackson Memorial Cemetery in Lexington, Virginia. Jackson was 39 when he died. His wife, Mary Anna Jackson, never remarried and was known as "the Widow of the Confederacy" until her death in 1915 at the age of 83. She is buried next to her husband. (LOC.)

Col. Robert E. Lee, the most prominent resident of Alexandria County, was offered command of the Union army on April 18, 1861, but declined. He left his home at Arlington House for the last time on April 22 and accepted command of the Virginia forces. Lee was to become the Confederacy's most successful and famous general. (LOC.)

After the war, from October 1865 until his death in 1870, Lee served as the president of Washington College (now Washington and Lee University) in Lexington, Virginia. Lee became a symbol of reconciliation between the North and South. He is buried at the Lee Chapel in Lexington (seen here). (LOC.)

James Ewell Brown "Jeb" Stuart was the Confederacy's most dashing cavalry officer. Dressed in a resplendent uniform, plumed hat, and cape, the flamboyant Stuart led the cavalry of the Army of Northern Virginia in many daring fights and raids. Union major general John Sedgwick called him "the greatest cavalry officer ever foaled in America." (LOC.)

The 31-year-old General Stuart was killed at the Battle of Yellow Tavern in May 1864. A bullet struck Stuart in the left side. This 1865 photograph shows the grave of Gen. J.E.B. Stuart (1833–1864) at Richmond, Virginia's, Hollywood Cemetery. The temporary marker seen here was replaced after the war. (LOC.)

Six hundred Confederate soldiers died in Warrenton field hospitals following the Battles of First and Second Manassas. The grave of each soldier was originally identified with a wooden marker bearing his name. These wooden markers had been made by local schoolchildren. During the Federal occupation of Warrenton, Union soldiers pulled up the wooden markers and burned them for firewood. The names of the soldiers buried at Warrenton were lost to history. The unknown remains were reburied after the war in a common grave marked by an imposing monument. In 1982, Robert E. Smith of Illinois, while doing genealogical research, discovered a box of records from the Warrenton field hospitals that had been misfiled in the National Archives. This accidental discovery led to the identification of 520 of the 600 soldiers whose remains are buried in Warrenton's mass grave. (AC.)

After the war, many local communities organized days of remembrance for the dead. In 1868, Union veterans adopted May 30 "for the purpose of strewing with flowers or otherwise decorating the graves of comrades who died in defense of their country," in the words of the Grand Army of the Republic. Many Southern states recognized Confederate Memorial Day on different dates, reflecting persistent sectional differences. (LOC.)

Monuments to the Civil War dead were erected in towns and cities across the North and South. Seen here is the Confederate Monument in Alexandria, Virginia, erected in 1889. An inscription on the north side of the base reads, "They died in the consciousness of duty faithfully performed." (LOC.)

In July 1911, Manassas hosted a peace jubilee to mark the 50th anniversary of the Civil War's first great battle. George Carr Round, a Union veteran who settled in Manassas, is credited with this gesture of reconciliation. The day was capped off by an address by President Taft. (LOC.)

Many veterans' groups sprang up in the South after the war. In 1889, a national organization called the United Confederate Veterans was formed. The purpose of the group was not to stir up old hatreds but to foster "social, literary, historical, and benevolent" ends. Confederate veterans are seen here at the Confederate Memorial at Arlington National Cemetery. (LOC.)

Pictured is the grave of a Confederate veteran. The United Confederate Veterans grew rapidly throughout the 1890s. Some 1,555 local organizations (called camps) were represented at the 1898 reunion. In 1911, an estimated crowd of 106,000 members and guests attended one reunion. Meetings continued until 1950, when only one member could attend. (AC.)

Established in 1866, the Grand Army of the Republic was a fraternal organization of Union veterans. This photograph shows Union veterans marching at the 36th National Encampment of the Grand Army of the Republic in Washington, DC, in October 1902. The organization disbanded in 1956 with the death of the last Union veteran. (LOC.)

The grave of Horace E. Ward (1839–1906) is at Arlington National Cemetery. Ward's affiliation with the Grand Army of the Republic is carved on his gravestone. The last Union veteran, Willard Woolson, died in 1956 at the age of 106. Woolson was a drummer boy. The last Union combat soldier, James Hard, died in 1953 at the age of 109. Claims and counterclaims swirl around the age and status of the last veterans, both Union and Confederate. The last verifiable Confederate veteran is thought to have been Pleasant Riggs Crump (1847–1951), although several men subsequently claimed to be the "oldest" Confederate soldier. Crump was from Alabama and served at the Siege of Petersburg. The last American slave is thought to have been Sylvester Magee, who died in 1971 at the purported age of 130. There is no birth certificate to verify his birth date. (AC.)

DISCOVER THOUSANDS OF LOCAL HISTORY BOOKS FEATURING MILLIONS OF VINTAGE IMAGES

Arcadia Publishing, the leading local history publisher in the United States, is committed to making history accessible and meaningful through publishing books that celebrate and preserve the heritage of America's people and places.

Find more books like this at
www.arcadiapublishing.com

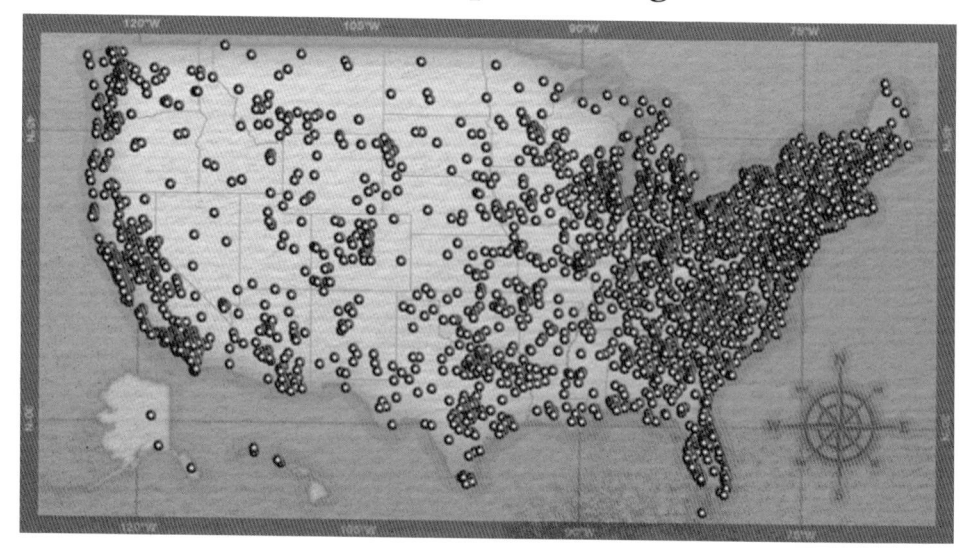

Search for your hometown history, your old stomping grounds, and even your favorite sports team.

Consistent with our mission to preserve history on a local level, this book was printed in South Carolina on American-made paper and manufactured entirely in the United States. Products carrying the accredited Forest Stewardship Council (FSC) label are printed on 100 percent FSC-certified paper.

MADE IN THE USA